Directory of Leading U.S. Export Management Companies

THIRD EDITION

Bergano Book Co./Johnston International Publishing Co.

The information contained in this book has been obtained from detailed questionnaires and telephone interviews. Since not all Export Management Companies in the U.S. returned questionnaires, this Directiory does not claim to list every U.S. Export Management Company.

While every effort has been made to verify and report the information as accurately as possible, neither the editors nor the publisher can be held responsible for inacccuracies and/or omissions which may exist in this book.

Published by Bergano Book Co. and Johnston International Publishing Co.

Copyright 1991 by Bergano Book Co. and Johnston International Publishing Co. Manufactured in the United States of America.

Library of Congress Catalog Card Number 90-82173
ISBN 0-917408-05-5

INTRODUCTION

THE EXPORT MANAGEMEMENT COMPANY -
Your Key to International Markets

by Bob Snyder, Group Publisher, Johnston International Publishing Co.,
and Adrienne Fishman, Director, Bergano Book Co.

An Export Management Company ("EMC") serves as the export department of a manufacturer, or as an extension of that department. An EMC provides a full range of export services, including identifying buyers and sellers, marketing and sales promotion, attending trade shows, providing technical product support, shipping, and sometimes even extending export credit.

The *Directory of Leading U.S. Export Mangement Companies,* co-published by Johnston International Publishing Co. and Bergano Book Co., gives you America's most definitive look at companies in the forefront of exporting - companies that represent America's most knowledgeable group of international traders.

What is an EMC?

An EMC is distinguishable from an "export consultant." Although the EMC may very well offer consulting services, the EMC's direct involvement in managing the buying and selling of product is the key distinction.

Yet an EMC is not solely "commodity-oriented," as is either the export trading company or the international distributor. The EMC generally bundles value-added marketing services with its sales efforts and most often works on "exclusive arrangements" with the manufacturers it represents. (Sometimes these "exclusive arrangements" can be narrowly defined, either geographically or by models. Nonetheless, an EMC's concern for working directly with the manufacturer clearly contrasts with the habits of export/import commodity traders.)

Several types of EMCs exist and each provides different services to help manufacturers from feeling like innocents abroad. Some EMCs specialize by product category (e.g. computers, automotive products) while others focus on an entire geographic region or just one country. Some will work only as an exclusively appointed official representative of the manufacturer; others have a range of products including some product lines which are not on an exclusive basis.

You will encounter EMCs that are no more than one-man bands, and others that have an extensive network of overseas offices. Sales volume can be as large as a small manufacturer's turnover or as low as one person's salary. It is important not to overvalue staff size - one person with extensive international contacts can move a lot of product - and, it may take only one person with the right contacts to conclude a $6 milllion deal in Abu Dhabi.

Which manufacturers should use an EMC?

Commonly, EMCs are associated with small or medium sized manufacturers, manufacturers who find overseas business intimidating or who simply don't have the time, means or financial resources to cope with a consistent export marketing plan. If you have a product which you think is exportable, yet which you are not now exporting in a consistent fashion, then you should contact some of the EMCs listed in this *Directory*. EMCs can be a valuable addition to practically any manufacturer's international marketing efforts.

Even manufacturers with extensive overseas distribution channels and subsidiaries can profit from export management companies. Large companies with an international vice president and several regional managers have successfully used EMCs in parts of the world where they lack on-the-ground export sales power (for example, in the Caribbean or Africa). All international sales directors should acquaint themselves with EMCs in their industry and ask the all-important question: "What can you do for my sales that I can't do myself?"

Start-up companies, particularly high-tech, are turning towards EMCs for an overseas "jump-start." Exporting can carry a lot of unknowns for start-ups; EMCs already have established contacts so they can speed up manufacturers' exporting cycles. For a start-up, this often supplies cash on a faster basis than domestic sales. Another reason start-ups are exporting from the beginning is on the advice of venture capitalists who recognize that competing in the global market is essential for some industries. A Bank of Boston study concluded that start-ups who begin to export within six months of shipping their first product have a statistically better chance of being in business five years later.

How manufacturers select and work with an EMC

Look for an EMC that handles products related to, but not competing with yours. If you want to export tires, talk to an EMC that exports cars and trucks. The experience need not be in exactly the same product category, but should be in a related category.

Decide how much control you want to retain over your product; this will be limited by your desire and ability to play a role in the export marketing. Some EMCs can take charge of your international advertising, service, or research, but the degree of involvement is negotiable with the individual EMC.

Decide in advance on the amount of feedback or reporting that you want. Will you be an active or passive partner? EMCs can work either way, but you should decide this up front.

Be comfortable with the EMC's size, method of specialization (product, industry, territory) and its management.

Discuss the financial arrangements and commit these to writing. Some EMCs work on commission alone, while others require a retainer plus commission. The size of the retainer depends upon the services expected. The percent of commission can vary according to the expected sales volume.

Interview a variety of EMCs, just as you would interview a potential advertising agency, consultant or accountant. Ask for references and contact them.

Once you have chosen one or more export management companies, negotiate a contract. Contract terms are normally two to five years to give EMCs the time needed to develop the international business and get a return on their investment of effort. Termination clauses often allow a 90-day out, sometimes based on a performance clause. Have the contract reviewed by an attorney experienced in international trade.

How EMCs help overseas buyers

Without EMCs, many American products would simply never find their way to overseas markets. Overseas buyers should acquaint themselves with a range of EMCs to open up access to new products. EMCs cater to the overseas buyers' needs and generally understand the buyers' problems better than most American manufacturers. (Many EMCs even employ citizens of the countries they export to, in order to gain local understanding.)

EMCs can often serve as "bellwethers." They can let the overseas buyer know about important product trends because they follow global market trends. Often an EMC will be responsible for bringing its customer into a whole new area of business - and with great success - because the EMC has already witnessed the success of this new product category in another country. Market and product consulting go hand-in-hand with an EMC's business.

EMCs can be very useful in arranging financing and finding the right way through complicated U.S. government export regulations.

Perhaps one of the benefits is the "style" of EMC selling. It's no secret that international business is a "people" business and the EMC develops much more of a family approach to his customers than does a manufacturer. This approach leads to better service and an in-depth international business friendship that can last for years.

How to use this *Directory*

If you are an OVERSEAS BUYER, here are the most export-minded companies in America who can help you buy better! Check the listings carefully for a description of the services and products offered. Find the company that matches your needs. Then contact the EMC - be sure to mention its listing in this book - and introduce yourself.

If you are a MANUFACTURER, review this book carefully. Some EMCs are supplying more of a commodity-sell, while others are providing value-added services. Feel free to contact all the EMCs listed here to solicit their business. Write a short letter and send your brochure and export price list, if you have one State your sales goals and ask the EMC how his company could assist. Be sure to find out about the specific financial arrangements. (If you need assistance, fax Bob Snyder at Johnston International Publishing Co., (708) 803-3328, for a sample form with which to approach an EMC.)

If you are an EMC, this issue will serve as a guide to your compatriots. Save this *Directory* in case you need to make a strategic alliance. Additionally, this issue is a great promotion for any EMC's business.

If you are an EXPORT SERVICE PROVIDER and wish to mail to all the EMCs in this book, why bother doing data entry? We can supply you with pressure-sensitive labels ready-to-mail for $125.00. Call Bergano Book Co. at (203) 254-2054.

This *Directory* is arranged so that you can locate EMCs three ways:

1. Geographically (EMCs are listed in state order, beginning on page 1)
2. By product category (see complete list of product categories on page 120; index begins on page 122)
3. Alphabetically by EMC's name, beginning on page 149.

In addition, as an added service to companies seeking to develop their export business, a "Consultants" section begins on page 109. These consultants to exporters may fill a specialized niche, such as offering assistance with government regulations, or developing export software, or may be more generalized, providing EMC services but on a more limited basis than an EMC.

When your relationship with an EMC begins, be sure top management is behind your export efforts. Full cooperation on your end will be to your own benefit. Understand that patience and perseverance are required. Personal meetings with your EMC will foster cooperation between you. By having an EMC that's right for you, and providing a good product, on time, you will see sales and profits increase as you become a global exporter.

TABLE OF CONTENTS

Vensamar Export Management
P. O. Box 7311
Huntsville, AL 35807

Phone: (205) 837-3007
Fax: (205) 837-9212

Contact: Johan A. Dijkhoffz, President
Year Established: 1986

Foreign language capabilities: Spanish, Dutch, Arabic
Geographic specialization: Europe, South America, Austral/Asia

Provides EMC services for:
computers, peripherals, business equipment and software; hardware.

Rizzo, Joseph F. Company
7436 East Stetson Dr., Suite 180
Scottsdale, AZ 85251-3517

Phone: (602) 990-3300
Fax: (602) 990-2907
Telex 249974 EXPO UR

Contact: Mary Ann F. Rizzo, President
Year Established: 1937

Foreign language capabilities: Italian, French, Spanish, German, Portuguese
Geographic specialization: Worldwide

Provides EMC services for:
accessories, luggage and jewelry; machinery and supplies; teflon semi-manufactures.

Wiesman & Company, Inc.
1916 East Fort Lowell Road
Tucson, AZ 85719

Phone: (602) 323-1760
Fax: (602) 881-6304
Telex 666479   *Cables:* WIEXCO

Contact: Benjamin E. Wiesman, President
Year Established: 1966

Foreign language capabilities: Spanish, French, Portuguese, German, Italian
Geographic specialization: Latin America, Caribbean

Provides EMC services for:
automobiles, accessories or parts; building materials; communication equipment and systems; consumer service industries: specialized machinery and equipment; farm equipment and products; heating, air-conditioning and refrigeration; industrial products and equipment; machinery and supplies; marine and related products; materials handling equipment; mining equipment, minerals and raw materials; paints, varnishes and enamels; safety and security equipment.

A B International
P. O. Box 410010
San Francisco, CA 94141-0010

Phone: (415) 421-7400
Fax: (415) 421-2392

Contact: Al Bolen, Partner

Year Established: 1977
Geographic specialization: Pacific Rim, Middle East

Provides EMC services for:
building materials; construction equipment; lighting; paints, varnishes and enamels; pipe fittings, valves, plumbing fixtures.

Abaco International Corp.

P. O. Box 4082
Irvine, CA 92716-4082
Phone: (714) 552-8494

Contact: Dale Martine, Export Coordinator
Year Established: 1959

Foreign language capabilities: German, French
Geographic specialization: Worldwide

Provides EMC services for:
apparel, textiles, garment components and leather goods; automobiles, accessories or parts; chemicals, chemical and petrochemical industries equipment and products; communication equipment and systems; computers, peripherals, business equipment and software; construction equipment; electrical, radio and TV, equipment and parts; food products and beverages; games, toys, etc.; household furnishings and appliances; medical equipment; sporting goods; men's and women's sportswear.

Amerasia Trading Co., Inc.

4546-B10 El Camino Real, Suite 172
Los Altos, CA 94023

Phone: (415) 967-2903
Fax: (415) 967-3014
Telex 176249 AAMI

Contact: Fred Salimi, Director
Year Established: 1981

Foreign language capabilities: French, Italian, Spanish, Indonesian, Farsi
Geographic specialization: Europe, Asia, Middle East, Far East, Mexico, Brazil

Provides EMC services for:
aircraft, accessories or parts; building materials; chemicals, chemical and petrochemical industries equipment and products; communication equipment and systems; computers, peripherals, business equipment and software; construction equipment; industrial products and equipment; medical equipment; mining equipment, minerals and raw materials; pharmaceuticals and hospital supplies.

American Enterprise Co.

465 California St.
San Francisco, CA 94104

Phone: (415) 362-3556
Fax: (415) 986-3013
Telex 278-298   *Cables:* AMENT

Contact: Bruce Park, President
Year Established: 1979

Foreign language capabilities: Japanese, Korean, Chinese
Geographic specialization: Far East, Middle East

Provides EMC services for:
food processing/packaging machinery and equipment; food products and beverages.

American Export Trading Co.

10919 Van Owen St.
N. Hollywood, CA 91605

Phone: (818) 985- 5114
Fax: (818) 985-5771
Telex 4973015 AMEXPO

Contact: Ben Epstein, Vice President, Marketing
Year Established: 1985

Foreign language capabilities: Russian, Spanish, Hebrew, Italian
Geographic specialization: Worldwide

Provides EMC services for:
aircraft, accessories or parts; automobiles, accessories or parts; building materials; construction equipment; consumer service industries: specialized machinery and equipment; electrical, radio and TV, equipment and parts; farm equipment and products; medical equipment; marine and related products; mining equipment, minerals and raw materials; pharmaceuticals and hospital supplies; safety and security equipment; trucks, accessories or parts.

American International Pacific Industries

1043 Avenida Acaso
Camarillo, CA 93010

Phone: (805) 388-7900
Fax: (805) 388-7950

Contact: J. R. Zimmerman, Int'l Marketing Director
Year Established: 1978

Foreign language capabilities: Spanish
Geographic specialization: Worldwide

Provides EMC services for:
automobiles, accessories or parts.

Amtrade International Corp.

6428 Sombrero Ave.
Cypress, CA 90630

Phone: (714) 892-9992
Fax: (714) 895-4818
Telex 655377

Contact: Michael R. Granat, President
Year Established: 1977

Foreign language capabilities: Spanish, German, Farsi
Geographic specialization: Worldwide

Provides EMC services for:
automobiles, accessories or parts; building materials; chemicals, chemical and petrochemical industries equipment and products; computers, peripherals, business equipment and software; construction equipment; farm equipment and products; food products and beverages; hardware; household furnishings and appliances; industrial products and equipment; medical equipment; marine and related products; sporting goods; swimming pool and spa equipment. Also offers export training programs.

Anaheim Marketing International

4332 E. La Palma Ave.
Anaheim, CA 92807

Phone: (714) 993-1702
Fax: (714) 993-1930
Telex 510 601 6554

Contact: Richard E. Meyerhoff, Marketing Manager

Year Established: 1985
Geographic specialization: Worldwide

Provides EMC services for:
air and water purification, pollution control and environmental control products and equipment; building materials; food processing/packaging machinery and equipment; household furnishings and appliances; marine and related products; pharmaceuticals and hospital supplies; restaurant, hotel and catering equipment.

Atlas Asia-Pacific

851 Burlway Rd.
Burlingame, CA 94010

Phone: (415) 347-3691
Fax: (415) 340-8739
Telex 331353 A/B ATLASCO BRGM
Cables: "ATLASCO" - Burlingame

Contact: William A. Ryan, President

Provides EMC services for:
automobiles, accessories or parts; chemicals, chemical and petrochemical industries equipment and products; trucks, accessories or parts.

Avalon Group, Ltd.
2659 Townsgate Rd., Suite 104
Westlake Village, CA 91361

Phone: (805) 495-5412
Fax: (805) 495-7546
Telex 299353 POST UR

Contact: D. Odom, Sales
Year Established: 1984

Foreign language capabilities: Arabic, French
Geographic specialization: Middle East,
People's Republic of China

Provides EMC services for:
aircraft, accessories or parts; building materials;
construction equipment; food products and
beverages; furniture; gasolines, lubricants, and
equipment; hardware; industrial products and
equipment; optical, photographic, and scientific
instruments; paints, varnishes and enamels; safety
and security equipment; testing equipment;
manufactured housing; aviation raw materials.

Bay World Trading, Ltd.
5 Third St., Hearst Bldg. 1018
San Francisco, CA 94103

Phone: (415) 979-0656
Fax: (415) 979-0336
Telex 312 0051 MCI UW

Contact: Bradley C. Mart, COO
Year Established: 1985

Foreign language capabilities: Spanish, French,
Arabic, Tagalog, Mandarin
Geographic specialization: Worldwide

Provides EMC services for:
building materials; computers, peripherals,
business equipment and software; food products
and beverages; medical equipment;
pharmaceuticals and hospital supplies.

Berkowitz, N. C. & Company
1095 Market St.
San Francisco, CA 94103

Phone: (415) 255-9781
Fax: (415) 255-9392
Telex 278227

Contact: Nathaniel Berkowitz, Director
Year Established: 1958

Foreign language capabilities: Spanish
Geographic specialization: Worldwide

Provides EMC services for:
air and water purification, pollution control and
environmental control products and equipment;
aircraft, accessories or parts; chemicals, chemical
and petrochemical industries equipment and
products; communication equipment and systems;
computers, peripherals, business equipment and
software; machinery and supplies; medical
equipment; marine and related products; materials
handling equipment; testing equipment. Also
provides consulting services.

Bisho, J. R. Co., Inc.
564 Market St.
San Francisco, CA 94104

Phone: (415) 397-0767
Fax: (415) 397-0835
Telex 470389
Cables: "SERVICE" SAN FRANCISCO

Contact: Joseph R. Bisho, President
Year Established: 1955

Foreign language capabilities: Chinese, Dutch
Geographic specialization: Pacific Rim, South &
Central America, Middle East, Europe

Provides EMC services for:
automobiles, accessories or parts; farm equipment
and products; marine and related products;
materials handling equipment; mining equipment,
minerals and raw materials; trucks, accessories or
parts; California wines; tractor parts.

Chaco International, Inc.

P. O. Box 700
Menlo Park, CA 94026

Phone: (408) 629-4800
Fax: (408) 365-9400

Contact: Luke Alexander, President
Year Established: 1978

Foreign language capabilities: Spanish
Geographic specialization: Worldwide

Provides EMC services for:
construction equipment; mining equipment, minerals and raw materials.

Continental Enterprises

7412 Count Circle
Huntington Beach, CA 92647

Phone: (714) 841-1403
Fax: (714) 843-2047
Telex (TWX) 910-596-1806

Contact: Luis Lopez, Director
Year Established: 1967

Foreign language capabilities: French, Spanish
Geographic specialization: Mexico, Spain, Middle East

Provides EMC services for:
air and water purification, pollution control and environmental control products and equipment; heating, air-conditioning and refrigeration. Provides export trading company services.

Eagle International Enterprises, Inc.

1415 Rollins Rd., Suite 4
Burlingame, CA 94014

Phone: (415) 340-8744
Fax: (415) 340-9290
Telex 499-6186 JENNIKE

Contact: Valmar C. Figueiredo, President
Year Established: 1980

Foreign language capabilities: Portuguese, Spanish
Geographic specialization: South & Central America, Asia

Provides EMC services for:
air and water purification, pollution control and environmental control products/equip.; aircraft, accessories or parts; automobiles, accessories or parts; building materials; chemicals, chemical and petrochemical industries equip. and products; construction equip.; farm equip. and products; food processing/ packaging machinery and equip.; food products/beverages; gasolines, lubricants, and equip.; heating, AC and refrigeration; industrial products and equip.; medical equip.; mining equip., minerals and raw materials; pharmaceuticals and hospital supplies; trucks, accessories or parts.

G.D.E., Inc.

187 W. Orangethorpe Ave., Unit 0
Placentia, CA 92670

Phone: (714) 528-6880
Fax: (714) 528-2734
Telex 910-592-1221

Contact: M.R. Rodriguez, President
Year Established: 1980

Foreign language capabilities: Portuguese, Spanish, French
Geographic specialization: Latin & South America

Provides EMC services for:
communication equipment and systems; computers, peripherals, business equipment and software; machinery and supplies; materials handling equipment; testing equipment.

Gladex Corporation

P. O. Box 1523
San Francisco, CA 94101

Phone: (415) 668-5286
Fax: (415) 668-0436
Cables: GLADIX SFO

Contact: Philip Heald, Vice President
Year Established: 1974

Foreign language capabilities: Chinese, German, Russian, Spanish, Japanese
Geographic specialization: Asia, Latin America, Eastern Europe

Provides EMC services for:
aircraft, accessories or parts; building materials; construction equipment; farm equipment and products; graphic arts, printing equipment and supplies; industrial products and equipment; medical equipment; marine and related products; mining equipment, minerals and raw materials; public utilities; restaurant, hotel and catering equipment; testing equipment; trucks, accessories or parts; military systems and equipment.

Global Merchandising Corp.

P. O. Box 410506
San Francisco, CA 94141-0506

Phone: (415) 285-8336
Fax: (415) 641-0952
Telex 278232 MROSS UR

Contact: James M. Connell, Export Trader
Year Established: 1957

Foreign language capabilities: Mandarin, Tagalog, French, Norwegian, Spanish, Portuguese
Geographic specialization: Pacific Rim

Provides EMC services for:
apparel, textiles, garment components and leather goods; automobiles, accessories or parts; building materials; food products and beverages; games, toys, etc.; heating, air-conditioning and refrigeration; sporting goods; testing equipment. Also provides export trading company services.

Global Technology, Inc.

1190 Mahala Place
Compton, CA 90220

Phone: (213) 635-7106
Fax: (213) 635-6301
Telex 910-346-6347

Contact: Chung P. Wang, Manager
Year Established: 1978

Foreign language capabilities: Chinese
Geographic specialization: Pacific Rim

Provides EMC services for:
audio-visual equipment and educational/training aids; communication equipment and systems; computers, peripherals, business equipment and software; consumer service industries: specialized machinery and equipment; electrical, radio and TV, equipment and parts.

Halprin International

3804 So. Broadway Place
Los Angeles, CA 90037

Phone: (213) 232-3131
Fax: (213) 232-2751

Contact: Lee A. Fishel, Export Manager
Year Established: 1948

Foreign language capabilities: Spanish, French, Arabic
Geographic specialization: Middle East, Far East, Latin & South America, Asia

Provides EMC services for:
safety and security equipment; fire fighting and safety equipment.

Hayden, Inc.
1531 Pomona Rd.
Corona, CA 91718-0848

Phone: (714) 736-2665 / (800) 854-4757
Fax: (714) 736-2658
Telex 709-159

Contact: Edward M. Johns, Vice President

Provides EMC services for:
automobiles, accessories or parts; trucks, accessories or parts.

Heritage International Inc.
2259 Torrance Blvd.
Torrance, CA 90501

Phone: (213) 328-1128
Fax: (213) 328-0115
Telex 677604 (TEMPOASIA GDNA)

Contact: Kenneth Miyamoto, President

Year Established: 1972

Geographic specialization: Australia, Orient

Provides EMC services for:
building materials; construction equipment; sporting goods; office accessories.

Holmes, Cecil Int'l Corp.
232 N. Locust St., Suite 3
Inglewood, CA 90301-1235

Phone: (213) 674-0572
Fax: (213) 677-3854

Contact: Cecil A. Holmes, Sr., President

Year Established: 1981

Geographic specialization: Far & Middle East, Central & South America, Africa, Canada

Provides EMC services for:
electrical, radio and TV, equipment and parts; food products and beverages; heating, air-conditioning and refrigeration; industrial products and equipment; materials handling equipment; mining equipment, minerals and raw materials.

Horn, John Stanley Co., Inc.
World Trade Center, Suite 340
San Francisco, CA 94111

Phone: (415) 781-6789
Fax: (415) 781-0629
Telex 470211

Contact: P. M. Horn, President
Year Established: 1955

Foreign language capabilities: Spanish, French, Italian, German
Geographic specialization: Europe, Pacific Rim

Provides EMC services for:
food products and beverages; restaurant, hotel and catering equipment.

Hypron, Inc.
2187 Garfias Drive
Pasadena, CA 91104-1897

Phone: (818) 797-2555
Fax: (818) 797-2555
Cables: HYPRON

Contact: Ernest Olsen, President
Year Established: 1973

Foreign language capabilities: Spanish,
Portuguese, French, Italian
Geographic specialization: Worldwide

Provides EMC services for:
safety and security equipment; time recorders and
systems.

IMEX Trading, Ltd.
3315 Como Lane
San Jose, CA 95118

Phone: (408) 264-2591
Fax: (503) 641-6059
Telex 4997145 IMEXSJ

Contact: Richard L. Kile, President
Year Established: 1974

Foreign language capabilities: French
Geographic specialization: Australia, New
Zealand, Canada, Central & South America

Provides EMC services for:
audio-visual equipment and educational/training
aids; automobiles, accessories or parts;
communication equipment and systems;
computers, peripherals, business equipment and
software; electrical, radio and TV, equipment and
parts; optical, photographic, and scientific
instruments; testing equipment.

Indamerica International, Inc.
4151 Beverly Blvd.
Los Angeles, CA 90004

Phone: (213) 663-2135
Fax: (213) 665-7462
Telex 4720794

Cables: INDAMERICA

Contact: Lorna Veliz

Geographic specialization: Worldwide

Provides EMC services for:
automobiles, accessories or parts.

INEX International
309 Cortsen Road
Pleasant Hill, CA 94523

Phone: (415) 937-6869
Fax: (415) 937-7678

Contact: Brian T. McConnell, President
Year Established: 1987

Foreign language capabilities: German, French,
Spanish, Chinese
Geographic specialization: Western & Eastern
Europe, Far East, China

Provides EMC services for:
communication equipment and systems;
computers, peripherals, business equipment and
software.

Intercontinental Enterprises Ltd.
256 So. Robertson, Suite 3194
Beverly Hills, CA 90211

Phone: (213) 276-6525 *Fax:* (213) 276-6595
Telex 6502920074 MCI

Contact: Gordon S. Riess, President
Year Established: 1976

Foreign language capabilities: French, German,
Spanish, Italian, Dutch, Swedish, Danish, Greek,
Japanese, Chinese, Portuguese
Geographic specialization: North & South
America, Europe, Asia/Pacific, Australia

Provides EMC services for:
air and water purification, pollution control and
environmental control products and equipment;
food products and beverages; games, toys, etc.;
medical equipment; optical, photographic, and
scientific instruments; pharmaceuticals and
hospital supplies; safety and security equipment;
sporting goods; testing equipment.

International Computer Systems
2156 Old Middlefield Way
Mountain View, CA 94043

Phone: (415) 940-1988
Fax: (415) 940-1949
Telex 296144 ELEC LTOS

Contact: Pirooz Binesh, Export Manager
Year Established: 1989

Foreign language capabilities: Swedish, Spanish,
Japanese, Farsi, Danish, Norwegian, Arabic,
Russian
Geographic specialization: Europe, Middle East, USSR

Provides EMC services for:
communication equipment and systems;
computers, peripherals, business equipment and
software.

International Product Marketing Group, Inc.
16123 Runnymede St.
Van Nuys, CA 91406-2952

Phone: (818) 781-1711
Fax: (818) 781-8842

Contact: Jay Dalton, President

Year Established: 1972
Geographic specialization: Europe, Africa, Asia

Provides EMC services for:
apparel, textiles, garment components and leather
goods; automobiles, accessories or parts;
chemicals, chemical and petrochemical industries
equipment and products; gasolines, lubricants, and
equipment; hardware; industrial products and
equipment; marine and related products; paints,
varnishes and enamels; sporting goods; testing
equipment; trucks, accessories or parts; jet-
powered racing cars.

L & W Equipment Corporation
1537 Pontius Ave.
Los Angeles, CA 90025

Phone: (213) 479-3911
Fax: (213) 479-6032
Telex 677668 LAWQUIP *Cables:* LAWQUIP

Contact: Maria Aragon
Year Established: 1967

Foreign language capabilities: Spanish, French
Geographic specialization: Pacific Rim, South
America, Middle East, Europe

Provides EMC services for:
building materials; electrical, radio and TV,
equipment and parts; heating, air-conditioning and
refrigeration; industrial products and equipment.
Performs export trading company services.

Lawrence, B. M. & Co.

450 Sansome St.
San Francisco, CA 94111

Phone: (415) 981-3650
Fax: (415) 981-2926
Telex 470171

Contact: R. Balmori, Vice President

Year Established: 1949

Geographic specialization: Worldwide

Provides EMC services for:
food products and beverages.

Mercatus International, Inc.

111 Central Avenue
Sausalito, CA 94965-2311

Phone: (415) 332-0501
Fax: (415) 332-1191

Contact: Peter Cregut, President
Year Established: 1986

Foreign language capabilities: French
Geographic specialization: Europe

Provides EMC services for:
communication equipment and systems; computers, peripherals, business equipment and software.

Meridian Group, The

13315 Washington Blvd., Suite 200
Los Angeles, CA 90066

Phone: (213) 306-6777
Fax: (213) 827-1160
Telex 677588

Contact: Christine Goffena, Marketing Manager
Year Established: 1960

Foreign language capabilities: Spanish, French
Geographic specialization: Worldwide

Provides EMC services for:
lighting; swimming pool and spa products, water filtration equipment.

Meridian Parts Corporation

5362 Production Dr.
Huntington Beach, CA 92605-3539

Phone: (714) 891-4444
Fax: (714) 893-6035
Telex 317707 MERIDIAN HB

Contact: Greg R. Walters, Asst. to the President

Provides EMC services for:
automobiles, accessories or parts.

Mirage Products International, Inc.

P. O. Box 11372
Beverly Hills, CA 90213

Phone: (213) 859-7348
Fax: (213) 858-8307

Contact: Alberto A. Yguico President
Year Established: 1978

Foreign language capabilities: Filipino, Spanish
Geographic specialization: Asia/Pacific

Provides EMC services for:
food products and beverages; games, toys, etc.;
pharmaceuticals and hospital supplies; safety and
security equipment.

Nelson, Edward International, Inc.

1180 So. Beverly Dr., Suite 505
Los Angeles, CA 90035

Phone: (213) 879-3050
Fax: (213) 553-9988
Telex 3720303 NELSONREP LSA

Contact: Edward G. Nelson, President
Year Established: 1963

Foreign language capabilities: German, French,
Spanish
Geographic specialization: Worldwide

Provides EMC services for:
games, toys, etc.; graphic arts, printing equipment
and supplies. Also functions as export sales
representatives and provides consulting services.

Niconor International Corporation

1686 Union St., Suite 203
San Francisco, CA 94123

Phone: (415) 771-0333
Fax: (415) 922-0149

Contact: Judithe Nicolai, President
Year Established: 1987

Foreign language capabilities: French, Spanish,
Italian, Portuguese, German
Geographic specialization: Europe, North & South
America

Provides EMC services for:
accessories, luggage and jewelry; apparel, textiles,
garment components and leather goods; food
products and beverages; contraceptives. Also
provides international translation services.

Oliver Resource Group, Inc.

4340 Redwood Hwy., Suite 150
San Rafael, CA 94903

Phone: (415) 492-9600
Fax: (415) 492-0449
Telex 4947237 TROP UI

Contact: James P. Oliver, President

Year Established: 1985

Geographic specialization: Worldwide

Provides EMC services for:
building materials; food products and beverages.
Also provides consulting and export trading
company services.

Orbis International, Ltd.
3301 El Camino Real, Suite 200
Atherton, CA 94027

Phone: (415) 367-6543
Fax: (415) 368-7717
Telex 910-250-6846
Cables: ORBIS VIA WUW

Contact: Roman Shukman, President
Year Established: 1985

Foreign language capabilities: Russian, Polish, German
Geographic specialization: USSR, Poland, Hungary

Provides EMC services for:
air and water purification, pollution control and environmental control products and equipment; automobiles, accessories or parts; communication equipment and systems; computers, peripherals, business equipment and software; construction equipment; farm equipment and products; food processing/packaging machinery and equipment; heating, air-conditioning and refrigeration; industrial products and equipment; machinery and supplies; medical equipment; mining equipment, minerals and raw materials; trucks, accessories or parts. Also provides consulting services.

Otis McAllister, Inc.
100 California St.
San Francisco, CA 94111

Phone: (415) 421-6010
Fax: (415) 421-6016
Telex RCA 278729
Cables: OTISMAC

Contact: Everett C. Golden III, Vice President
Year Established: 1892

Foreign language capabilities: Spanish
Geographic specialization: Central & Latin America, Caribbean, Europe, Asia

Provides EMC services for:
food products and beverages.

Overseas Operations Inc.
P. O. Box 7000-222
Redondo Beach, CA 90277-5779

Phone: (213) 540-4600
Fax: (213) 540-8382
Telex 4720134 WALDECKRNDO

Contact: Michele McGowan Exec. Vice President
Year Established: 1948

Foreign language capabilities: Spanish, French, German, Dutch, Italian
Geographic specialization: Worldwide

Provides EMC services for:
gasolines, lubricants, and equipment; hardware; heating, air-conditioning and refrigeration; household furnishings and appliances; lighting; safety and security equipment.

Pacific Commerce Co., Ltd.
14761-G Franklin Ave.
Tustin, CA 92680

Phone: (714) 731-2009
Fax: (714) 731-2912
Telex 151002

Contact: Gary Roberts, President
Year Established: 1973

Foreign language capabilities: Mandarin, Chinese
Geographic specialization: Pacific Rim

Provides EMC services for:
food products and beverages.

Pacific Exports

P. O. Box 3113
San Dimas, CA 91773

Phone: (714) 599-4424
Fax: (714) 599-8309
Telex 469462
Cables: PACEXP

Contact: Karl J. Ruzicka, Managing Director
Year Established: 1982

Foreign language capabilities: Spanish, French, German, Russian
Geographic specialization: Worldwide

Provides EMC services for:
farm equipment and products; machinery and supplies; irrigation equipment and supplies.

Pan Pacific International

24011 Plover Lane
Laguna Niguel, CA 92677

Phone: (714) 831-6518
Fax: (714) 831-5150

Contact: Harry Taw, President
Year Established: 1988

Foreign language capabilities: Chinese
Geographic specialization: Southeast Asia, Pacific Region

Provides EMC services for:
chemicals, chemical and petrochemical industries equipment and products; medical equipment; pharmaceuticals and hospital supplies.

Pierce International

1592 Castleview Court
Westlake Village, CA 91361

Phone: (805) 499-4329
Fax: (805) 498-0665
Telex 910-336-5441

Contact: Rollie A. Pierce, President
Year Established: 1986

Provides EMC services for:
aircraft, accessories or parts.

Provident Traders, Inc.

150 Spear St., Suite 1100
San Francisco, CA 94105

Phone: (415) 979-0577
Fax: (415) 957-1145

Contact: John Keevan-Lynch, President
Year Established: 1988

Foreign language capabilities: Spanish
Geographic specialization: Latin America

Provides EMC services for:
construction equipment; mining equipment, minerals and raw materials. Also provides consulting services.

Rebel, Albert & Associates, Inc.

166 University Parkway
Pomona, CA 91768

Phone: (714) 594-9515
Fax: (714) 594-2398
Telex 312762

Contact: Carl A. Telles, Vice President
Year Established: 1946

Foreign language capabilities: Spanish
Geographic specialization: Far East, Central &
South America

Provides EMC services for:
air and water purification, pollution control and
environmental control products and equipment;
food processing/packaging machinery and
equipment; heating, air-conditioning and
refrigeration; industrial products and equipment.

Regalis USA, Inc.

8361 Vickers St., Suite 203-208
San Diego, CA 92111

Phone: (619) 565-8485
Fax: (619) 565-1004

Contact: Henry Y. T. Chia, President
Year Established: 1983

Foreign language capabilities: Chinese, Malay
Geographic specialization: Pacific Rim

Provides EMC services for:
air and water purification, pollution control and
environmental control products and equipment;
automobiles, accessories or parts; communication
equipment and systems; food products and
beverages; games, toys, etc.; hardware;
household furnishings and appliances; optical,
photographic, and scientific instruments;
pharmaceuticals and hospital supplies; restaurant,
hotel and catering equipment; sporting goods;
trucks, accessories or parts. Also provides
consulting services and import functions.

RHA Group

23455 Madero, Unit C
Mission Viejo, CA 92720

Phone: (714) 581-9373
Fax: (714) 581-9592

Contact: Paul H. Armstrong, President
Year Established: 1989

Foreign language capabilities: Russian, Spanish,
Portuguese
Geographic specialization: USSR, Peru

Provides EMC services for:
apparel, textiles, garment components and leather
goods; communication equipment and systems;
computers, peripherals, business equipment and
software; electrical, radio and TV, equipment and
parts; medical equipment.

Romac Export Management Corp.

2242 So. Hobart Blvd.
Los Angeles, CA 90018-2149

Phone: (213) 734-2922
Fax: (213) 732-4087
Telex 910-321-4657 ROMAC. EXPORT
Cables: NUWESTMRKT, LOS ANGELES, CA

Contact: Roberta Best, Vice President
Year Established: 1978

Foreign language capabilities: Japanese, French
Geographic specialization: Western Europe, UK,
Japan

Provides EMC services for:
accessories, luggage and jewelry; apparel, textiles,
garment components and leather goods; food
products and beverages; furniture; games, toys,
etc.; graphic arts, printing equipment and supplies;
hardware; household furnishings and appliances;
lighting; marine and related products; restaurant,
hotel and catering equipment; safety and security
equipment; sporting goods; fine art, crafts and
antiques; fine handmade products.

Row International, Inc.
105 Hill Top Dr.
Los Gatos, CA 95032

Phone: (408) 356-2418
Fax: (408) 356-1683
Telex 287561

Contact: A. M. Fletcher, Vice President - Sales
Year Established: 1974

Foreign language capabilities: Spanish, German
Geographic specialization: Spain, UK, Australia, New Zealand, Middle East, Singapore, Hong Kong

Provides EMC services for:
communication equipment and systems; computers, peripherals, business equipment and software; electrical, radio and TV, equipment and parts; graphic arts, printing equipment and supplies; marine and related products; testing equipment.

Sacks, Harvey C., Export Consulting, Inc.
2811 Wilshire Blvd., Suite #615
Santa Monica, CA 90403

Phone: (213) 828-6294
Fax: (213) 828-0299

Contact: Harvey C. Sacks, President

Year Established: 1982

Geographic specialization: Western & Eastern Europe, USSR

Provides EMC services for:
audio-visual equipment and educational/training aids; chemicals, chemical and petrochemical industries equipment and products; communication equipment and systems; computers, peripherals, business equipment and software; optical, photographic, and scientific instruments; testing equipment. Also provides consulting services and functions as a trading company.

Saria International, Inc.
1200 Industrial Rd., Unit 2
San Carlos, CA 94070

Phone: (415) 591-1440
Fax: (415) 591-1976
Telex 171 944

Contact: A. Azem, President
Year Established: 1976

Foreign language capabilities: Spanish, French, Arabic
Geographic specialization: Worldwide

Provides EMC services for:
building materials; gasolines, lubricants, and equipment; hardware; heating, air-conditioning and refrigeration; industrial products and equipment; lighting; paints, varnishes and enamels; safety and security equipment.

Schmid, H. P. Inc.
P. O. Box 193707
San Francisco, CA 94119-3707

Phone: (415) 956-5811
Fax: (415) 956-1179
Telex 278284 HPS UR
Cables: SCHMID, SAN FRANCISCO

Contact: Hans P. Schmid, President
Year Established: 1978

Foreign language capabilities: Spanish, German, French, Dutch, Cantonese
Geographic specialization: Worldwide

Provides EMC services for:
food products and beverages.

Silicon International

85 Homer Lane
Menlo Park, CA 94025

Phone: (415) 854-6801
Fax: (415) 854-3008

Contact: P. Dietz, President

Year Established: 1988

Provides EMC services for:
communication equipment and systems;
computers, peripherals, business equipment and
software; electrical, radio and TV, equipment and
parts; testing equipment; semi-conductor
manufacturing equipment.

T A International, Inc.

270 S. Bristol St., Suite 101-103
Costa Mesa, CA 92626

Phone: (714) 556-6100
Fax: (714) 751-0114

Contact: Sy N. Nguyen, President
Year Established: 1986

Foreign language capabilities: Vietnamese
Geographic specialization: Southeast Asia

Provides EMC services for:
medical equipment; pharmaceuticals and hospital
supplies; dental supplies and equipment.

Taico Trading Corporation

1453 Mission St.
San Francisco, CA 94103-2577

Phone: (415) 863-1506
Fax: (415) 863-0939   *Cables:* AMERICIMP

Contact: F. S. Dickson, Export Manager
Year Established: 1894

Foreign language capabilities: French, Spanish,
Italian
Geographic specialization: Worldwide

Provides EMC services for:
marine and related products; sporting goods;
fishing tackle; camping equipment; shooting and
hunting accessories; pet supplies. Also performs
export trading company functions.

Trade Development Corp. of Chicago

2049 Century Place E., Suite 416
Los Angeles, CA 90067

Phone: (213) 556-8091
Fax: (213) 556-3088
Telex 910-221-0054   *Cables:* MICHWADE

Contact: Michael R. A. Wade, President
Year Established: 1979

Foreign language capabilities: Chinese,
Japanese, Korean
Geographic specialization: China, Japan, Pacific
Region

Provides EMC services for:
aircraft, accessories or parts; automobiles,
accessories or parts; communication equipment
and systems; computers, peripherals, business
equipment and software; construction equipment;
electrical, radio and TV, equipment and parts; farm
equipment and products; food processing/
packaging machinery and equipment; industrial
products and equipment; machinery and supplies;
medical equipment; optical, photographic, and
scientific instruments; testing equipment. Also
performs market research.

Tradex International, Inc.
230 Newport Center Dr., Suite 250
Newport Beach, CA 92660

Phone: (714) 752-4077
Fax: (714) 720-4077

Contact: Kenneth L. Nicolas, CEO
Year Established: 1968

Foreign language capabilities: German, French, Dutch, Hungarian, Spanish
Geographic specialization: Western & Eastern Europe

Provides EMC services for:
aircraft, accessories or parts; automobiles, accessories or parts; chemicals, chemical and petrochemical industries equipment and products; computers, peripherals, business equipment and software; farm equipment and products; gasolines, lubricants, and equipment; heating, air-conditioning and refrigeration; machinery and supplies; medical equipment; mining equipment, minerals and raw materials. Handles all types of products and provides consulting services.

Triple Gold Trading Inc.
130 Battery St., Suite 350
San Francisco, CA 94111

Phone: (415) 677-9888
Fax: (415) 399-9493

Contact: Louisa Chiu, Office Manager
Year Established: 1989

Foreign language capabilities: Mandarin, Cantonese and other Chinese languages
Geographic specialization: Asia

Provides EMC services for:
metal scrap.

United Exporters Co.
1095 Market St.
San Francisco, CA 94103

Phone: (415) 255-9393
Fax: (415) 255-9392

Contact: Myra Berkowitz, President
Year Established: 1953

Foreign language capabilities: French, Dutch
Geographic specialization: New Zealand, Asia, Europe

Provides EMC services for:
computers, peripherals, business equipment and software; medical equipment; marine and related products; testing equipment.

United Gulf Services, Inc.
2659 Townsagate Rd., Suite 104
Westlake Village, CA 91361

Phone: (805) 496-9311
Fax: (805) 495-7546
Telex 299353 POST UR

Contact: R. M. Habib, Vice President
Year Established: 1977

Foreign language capabilities: Arabic, French, Spanish
Geographic specialization: Middle East, North Africa, Europe

Provides EMC services for:
aircraft, accessories or parts; building materials; construction equipment; food products and beverages; furniture; gasolines, lubricants, and equipment; hardware; industrial products and equipment; optical, photographic, and scientific instruments; paints, varnishes and enamels; safety and security equipment; testing equipment; manufactured housing; aviation raw materials.

Worldwide Exporters, Inc.
2633 Manhattan Beach Blvd.
Redondo Beach, CA 90278

Phone: (213) 536-0062
Fax: (213) 536-9796
Telex 650-276-3587 MCIUW

Contact: Scott Manhard, President

Geographic specialization: Pacific Rim

Provides EMC services for:
air and water purification, pollution control and environmental control products and equipment; communication equipment and systems; computers, peripherals, business equipment and software; food processing/packaging machinery and equipment; graphic arts, printing equipment and supplies; heating, air-conditioning and refrigeration; industrial products and equipment; optical, photographic, and scientific instruments; testing equipment.

Worldwide Trade Opportunities, Inc.
7770 Regents Road, Suite 370
San Diego, CA 92122

Phone: (619) 552-1400
Fax: (619) 552-8484
Telex 1561628

Contact: Steven A. Freed, President

Year Established: 1973

Geographic specialization: Worldwide

Provides EMC services for:
air and water purification, pollution control and environmental control products and equipment; apparel, textiles, garment components and leather goods; automobiles, accessories or parts; chemicals, chemical and petrochemical industries equipment and products; computers, peripherals, business equipment and software; industrial products and equipment; medical equipment; paints, varnishes and enamels; pharmaceuticals and hospital supplies; safety and security equipment; sporting goods; trucks, accessories or parts.

Yagi, S. Inc., dba Primex, Inc.
555 California St., Suite 5170
San Francisco CA 94104

Phone: (415) 956-4097
Fax: (415) 956-5591
Telex 278399

Contact: Jack Yagi, President
Year Established: 1981

Foreign language capabilities: Japanese, French
Geographic specialization: Worldwide

Provides EMC services for:
building materials; chemicals, chemical and petrochemical industries equipment and products; farm equipment and products; food products and beverages; industrial products and equipment; mining equipment, minerals and raw materials; paints, varnishes and enamels; trucks, accessories or parts.

Ziegler Corporation, The
850 Battery St.
San Francisco, CA 94111

Phone: (415) 421-1345
Fax: (415) 421-1584
Telex 278350

Contact: John A. Ziegler, CEO

Year Established: 1972

Geographic specialization: Far East, Europe

Provides EMC services for:
food products and beverages.

Orion International & Company, Inc.
P. O. Box 3533
Littleton, CO 80161-3533

Phone: (303) 290-6050
Fax: (303) 290-6052
Telex 282880 ORION UR

Contact: Charles C. Pineo III, President
Year Established: 1986

Foreign language capabilities: German, Spanish, Turkish, Chinese
Geographic specialization: Europe, Mid & Far East

Provides EMC services for:
chemicals, chemical and petrochemical industries equipment and products; heating, air-conditioning and refrigeration; industrial products and equipment; medical equipment; mining equipment, minerals and raw materials; soap-making machinery.

Rocky Mountain Export Co., Inc.
P. O. Box 31773
Aurora, CO 80041

Phone: (303) 361-9422
Fax: (303) 364-1668
Telex 45766   *Cables:* ROMEXCO

Contact: Robert H. Reynolds, President
Year Established: 1941

Foreign language capabilities: Spanish, French, German
Geographic specialization: Worldwide

Provides EMC services for:
construction equipment.

Dage Corporation
911 Hope Street
Stamford, CT 06907-0385

Phone: (203) 324-3123
Fax: (203) 323-3563
Telex 82941 or 828828 DATUM UF

Contact: John Everett, Exec. Vice President
Year Established: 1946

Foreign language capabilities: Spanish, German, French, Russian, Portuguese
Geographic specialization: Agents in 35 Countries

Provides EMC services for:
communication equipment and systems; electrical, radio and TV, equipment and parts; hardware; industrial products and equipment; testing equipment; microwave components; satellite communication equipment.

Intrade, Inc.
P. O. Box 608
Litchfield, CT 06759

Phone: (203) 567-5901
Fax: (203) 567-5698
Telex 211441

Contact: Stephanie L. Wachman, Mktg. Mgr.
Year Established: 1964

Foreign language capabilities: French
Geographic specialization: Europe, Far East, Australia, New Zealand

Provides EMC services for:
electronic components.

Nesa Corporation

P. O. Box 5066
Brookfield, CT 06804

Phone: (203) 775-0578
Fax: (203) 775-0522
Telex 643763 NESACO BRKF

Contact: Richard E. Stanco, Managing Director
Year Established: 1979

Foreign language capabilities: Spanish, German
Geographic specialization: Worldwide

Provides EMC services for:
communication equipment and systems; electrical, radio and TV, equipment and parts; safety and security equipment.

Sibco, Inc.

87 Wedgemere Road
Stamford, CT 06905

Phone: (203) 322-4891
Fax: (203) 329-2671
Telex 6819185

Contact: S. J. (Sibby) Buccheri, President

Geographic specialization: Worldwide

Provides EMC services for:
automobiles, accessories or parts.

Torning International, Inc.

98 Lancaster Rd.
Glastonbury, CT 06033-0799

Phone: (203) 659-2349
Fax: (203) 633-6422

Contact: Ralph R. Torning, President
Year Established: 1985

Foreign language capabilities: German
Geographic specialization: Western Europe

Provides EMC services for:
aircraft, accessories or parts; electrical, radio and TV, equipment and parts; industrial products and equipment; machinery and supplies.

VIE International Inc.

P. O. Box 972
Glastonbury, CT 06033

Phone: (203) 659-1397
Fax: (203) 659-9679

Contact: Hugo E. Galarza, President
Year Established: 1980

Foreign language capabilities: Spanish
Geographic specialization: Latin America, Spain, Portugal, India

Provides EMC services for:
aircraft, accessories or parts; apparel, textiles, garment components and leather goods; automobiles, accessories or parts; chemicals, chemical and petrochemical industries equipment and products; computers, peripherals, business equipment and software; industrial products and equipment; machinery and supplies; mining equipment, minerals and raw materials; paints, varnishes and enamels; paper, packaging and containers; safety and security equipment; trucks, accessories or parts.

Beijing Trade Exchange, Inc.
700 E Street S.E.
Washington, DC 20003

Phone: (202) 546-5534
Fax: (202) 543-2488
Telex 197504 BTE WSH UT

Contact: John Canellakis, Vice President
Year Established: 1985

Foreign language capabilities: Chinese
Geographic specialization: China

Provides EMC services for:
accessories, luggage and jewelry; apparel, textiles, garment components and leather goods; audio-visual equipment and educational/training aids; computers, peripherals, business equipment and software; electrical, radio and TV, equipment and parts; safety and security equipment; sporting goods.

ITM Corporation
3421 M St., N.W., Suite 317
Washington, DC 20007

Phone: (703) 525-0110
Fax: (703) 525-0306
Telex 4972656FIGLTD

Contact: Charles Hrebenach, Operations Manager
Year Established: 1977

Foreign language capabilities: Spanish
Geographic specialization: Latin America, Europe, Asia

Provides EMC services for:
medical equipment; pharmaceuticals and hospital supplies.

Ajax International Corp.
P. O. Box 52-3736
Miami, FL 33152

Phone: (305) 592-1684
Fax: (305) 592-1820
Telex 80-3220
Cables: AJAXINT

Contact: Lino R. De La Hera, President

Foreign language capabilities: Spanish
Geographic specialization: Worldwide

Provides EMC services for:
automobiles, accessories or parts.

All American Commodities, Inc.
2501 Alt. 19, Suite B
Palm Harbor, FL 34683

Phone: (813) 786-5420
Fax: (813) 733-8671
Telex 4938448 DUNE MIA

Contact: Ward Lamber, President

Year Established: 1984
Geographic specialization: Caribbean, Central & South America

Provides EMC services for:
chemicals, chemical and petrochemical industries equipment and products; farm equipment and products.

Amas International, Inc.

4400 Ponce De Leon Blvd.
Coral Gables, FL 33146

Phone: (305) 446-6665
Fax: (305) 443-0308
Telex 51-9660
Cables: AMASINC

Contact: Rodger F. Schultz, President
Year Established: 1976

Foreign language capabilities: Spanish
Geographic specialization: Caribbean, Central &
South America, Africa, Europe

Provides EMC services for:
audio-visual equipment and educational/training
aids; furniture; gasolines, lubricants, and
equipment; graphic arts, printing equipment and
supplies; hardware; heating, air-conditioning and
refrigeration; household furnishings and
appliances; industrial products and equipment;
lighting; marine and related products; paper,
packaging and containers; public utilities; time
recorders and systems; tires.

Amed International

1929-31 Ponce De Leon Blvd.
Coral Gables, FL 33134-4412

Phone: (305) 448-6821
Fax: (305) 448-3224
Telex 80-3203 AMED INTL

Contact: Alexander S. Tar, President
Year Established: 1961

Foreign language capabilities: Spanish, German,
French, Hungarian
Geographic specialization: Worldwide

Provides EMC services for:
medical equipment. Also provides consulting
services.

Atlantech Inc.

6106 Courtside Drive
Bradenton, FL 34210

Phone: (813) 755-2434
Fax: (813) 755-4565

Contact: Joseph P. Vermeren, President
Year Established: 1987

Foreign language capabilities: Western European
languages
Geographic specialization: Western Europe,
Pacific Rim

Provides EMC services for:
automobiles, accessories or parts; communication
equipment and systems; computers, peripherals,
business equipment and software.

Automotive Export Inc.

P. O. Box 1925
Miami, FL 33138

Phone: (305) 379-1985
Fax: (305) 379-1528
Cables: AUTOEXPORT

Contact: Warren Katz, General Manager
Year Established: 1968

Foreign language capabilities: Spanish, German,
French, Dutch
Geographic specialization: Worldwide

Provides EMC services for:
automobiles, accessories or parts; industrial
products and equipment; trucks, accessories or
parts; tools; automobile chemicals.

Camex International, Inc.

8020 N.W. 14th St.
Miami, FL 33126

Phone: (305) 592-7276
Fax: (305) 592-0953
Telex 803570
Cables: CAMEXINT

Contact: Philip R. Lecours, President
Year Established: 1974

Foreign language capabilities: Spanish
Geographic specialization: Central & South
America, Caribbean, Persian Gulf area

Provides EMC services for:
audio-visual equipment and educational/training aids; medical equipment; pharmaceuticals and hospital supplies; safety and security equipment.

Cobo, J. & Associates, Inc.

2414 Coral Way
Miami, FL 33145

Phone: (305) 854-2501
Fax: (305) 856-1542
Telex 153225
Cables: COBOTEL

Contact: Juan A. Cobo, President
Year Established: 1974

Foreign language capabilities: Spanish, Portuguese
Geographic specialization: Caribbean, Central &
South America, Mexico

Provides EMC services for:
food processing/packaging machinery and equipment; restaurant, hotel and catering equipment; laundry equipment.

Colonial International Corp.- COINCO

7311 N.W. 12 St., Suite 11
Miami, FL 33126
Phone: (305) 592-1948

Contact: Werner Meier, President
Year Established: 1979

Foreign language capabilities: Spanish
Geographic specialization: Europe, Japan

Provides EMC services for:
apparel, textiles, garment components and leather goods; automobiles, accessories or parts; trucks, accessories or parts.

CPS Marketing Corp.

2000 Main Street, Suite 500, Barnett Centre
Fort Myers, FL 33901-3050

Phone: (813) 466-8343
Fax: (813) 332-7092
Telex 650-261-6968

Contact: Christian P. Swartz, President

Year Established: 1987
Geographic specialization: Europe, Latin America,
Asia/Pacific

Provides EMC services for:
aircraft, accessories or parts; computers, peripherals, business equipment and software; furniture; games, toys, etc.; medical equipment; pharmaceuticals and hospital supplies; restaurant, hotel and catering equipment.

Dibma Enterprises, Inc.
2510 S.W. 27th Ave.
Miami, FL 33133

Phone: (305) 567-9456
Fax: (305) 567-9808

Contact: Ismael Dominguez, Export Manager
Year Established: 1988

Foreign language capabilities: Spanish, Italian, French
Geographic specialization: Europe, Latin America

Provides EMC services for:
communication equipment and systems; computers, peripherals, business equipment and software; electrical, radio and TV, equipment and parts; telephones. Specializes in electronics.

E & G International, Inc.
3001 Ponce De Leon Blvd.
Coral Gables, FL 33134-6824

Phone: (305) 444-2541
Fax: (305) 442-1078
Telex 27-5399
Cables: EMERGO (CGBL)

Contact: Joseph B. Gomez, General Manager
Year Established: 1969

Foreign language capabilities: Spanish, French, Portuguese, Italian
Geographic specialization: Worldwide

Provides EMC services for:
industrial products and equipment; medical equipment; sporting goods; compressed gas, cylinders and cylinder valves.

Electrical Sales Corp. Int'l
16411 N.W. 8th Ave.
Miami, FL 33169

Phone: (305) 625-7669
Fax: (305) 624-9239
Telex 6811318 ESCORP

Contact: Kenneth M. Dreyfuss, President
Year Established: 1941

Foreign language capabilities: Spanish
Geographic specialization: Caribbean, Central America, Northern South America

Provides EMC services for:
electrical, radio and TV, equipment and parts; heating, air-conditioning and refrigeration; lighting; restaurant, hotel and catering equipment.

Euroscand, Inc.
14040 Leaning Pine Dr.
Miami Lakes, FL 33014

Phone: (305) 556-1085
Fax: (305) 557-3882

Contact: Goran Hellman, President
Year Established: 1979

Foreign language capabilities: Swedish, Norwegian, Danish, German
Geographic specialization: Sweden, Norway, Denmark, Finland

Provides EMC services for:
air and water purification, pollution control and environmental control products and equipment; heating, air-conditioning and refrigeration; medical equipment; sporting goods.

F. P. Intersales Corporation

P. O. Box 660980
Miami, FL 33266-0980

Phone: (305) 635-5726
Fax: (305) 635-5784

Contact: Fernando Perez, President
Year Established: 1972

Foreign language capabilities: Spanish
Geographic specialization: Central & South America, Caribbean

Provides EMC services for:
building materials; chemicals, chemical and petrochemical industries equipment and products; electrical, radio and TV, equipment and parts; food processing/packaging machinery and equipment; hardware; lighting; synthetic resin.

Global Marketing Services, Inc.

3643 Cortez Rd. West, Suite 150
Bradenton, FL 34210

Phone: (813) 751-6293
Fax: (813) 751-1900
Cables: GLOBAL MS BNTN

Contact: Stanley E. Schmidt, President
Year Established: 1982

Foreign language capabilities: French, Spanish
Geographic specialization: Worldwide

Provides EMC services for:
automobiles, accessories or parts; building materials; optical, photographic, and scientific instruments.

Gomez, Manuel and Associates, Inc.

P. O. Box 59-2162
Miami, FL 33159-2162

Phone: (305) 642-0311, (800)-825-5646
Fax: (305) 642-7912
Cables: TODOACOLOR MIA

Contact: Manual Gomez, Sr., Export Sales Mgr.
Year Established: 1963

Foreign language capabilities: Spanish, Portuguese
Geographic specialization: Worldwide

Provides EMC services for:
automobiles, accessories or parts; construction equipment; farm equipment and products; gasolines, lubricants, and equipment; marine and related products; trucks, accessories or parts.

Grable, John Exports, Inc.

3318 S.W. 2nd Ave.
Fort Lauderdale, FL 33315-3301

Phone: (305) 462-7977
Fax: (305) 462-7982

Contact: David W. Dunlevy, General Manager

Year Established: 1968
Geographic specialization: Bermuda, Caribbean, Central & South America, South Pacific

Provides EMC services for:
air and water purification, pollution control and environmental control products and equipment; building materials; construction equipment; hardware; lighting; paints, varnishes and enamels; plumbing, electrical, well supplies and pumps.

Haller, Mart Inc.

P. O. Box 140159
Coral Gables, FL 33114-0159

Phone: (305) 444-4617
Fax: (305) 445-7551
Telex 441692

Contact: Edwin P. Haller, President
Year Established: 1933

Foreign language capabilities: Spanish, Italian
Geographic specialization: Worldwide

Provides EMC services for:
air and water purification, pollution control and environmental control products and equipment; communication equipment and systems; electrical, radio and TV, equipment and parts; heating, air-conditioning and refrigeration.

Hemisol Export & Import Corp.

2103 Coral Way, Suite 110
Miami, FL 33145

Phone: (305) 856-1921
Fax: (305) 856-0544
Telex 810-848-4470

Contact: Simon Sol, Jr., Operations Manager
Year Established: 1982

Foreign language capabilities: Spanish
Geographic specialization: Caribbean, Central & South America

Provides EMC services for:
aircraft, accessories or parts; automobiles, accessories or parts; building materials; chemicals, chemical and petrochemical industries equipment and products; communication equipment and systems; construction equipment; electrical, radio and TV, equipment and parts; farm equipment and products; hardware; heating, air-conditioning and refrigeration; household furnishings and appliances; lighting; restaurant, hotel and catering equipment; trucks, accessories or parts.

Intertech Worldwide Corp.

4400 N. Federal Highway
Boca Raton, FL 33431

Phone: (407) 395-5441
Fax: (407) 395-5457
Telex 568683 INTERTECH

Contact: David A. Igdaloff, President
Year Established: 1977

Foreign language capabilities: French, Portuguese, Spanish, Japanese
Geographic specialization: Japan, South America

Provides EMC services for:
aircraft, accessories or parts; industrial products and equipment; machinery and supplies; medical equipment; materials handling equipment; restaurant, hotel and catering equipment. Provides services related to technology licensing.

Jason Marketing Corp.

11725 N.W. 100th Rd. #4
Medley, FL 33178

Phone: (305) 882-6716
Fax: (305) 882-6724
Telex 522998 JAMARK

Contact: Norman Welch, President
Year Established: 1979

Foreign language capabilities: Spanish
Geographic specialization: Caribbean, Central & South America

Provides EMC services for:
food products and beverages.

Lindeco International Corp.
1716 N.W. 82nd Ave.
Miami, FL 33126

Phone: (305) 477-4446
Fax: (305) 477-8116
Telex 620440

Contact: Enrique Escobar, Vice President
Year Established: 1957

Foreign language capabilities: Spanish, German
Geographic specialization: Worldwide

Provides EMC services for:
automobiles, accessories or parts; trucks, accessories or parts.

Micro Informatica Corp.
99 SE 5th Street, Suite 120
Miami, FL 33131

Phone: (305) 377-1930
Fax: (305) 377-0023

Contact: Maria Salgado, Sales Manager
Year Established: 1985

Foreign language capabilities: Portuguese, Spanish
Geographic specialization: South America, Europe

Provides EMC services for:
computers, peripherals, business equipment and software.

Parts Overseas Corporation
3600 N.W. 60th Street
Miami, FL 33142

Phone: (305) 633-8760
Fax: (305) 633-9617

Contact: Frank Fernandez, President
Year Established: 1986

Foreign language capabilities: Spanish
Geographic specialization: Caribbean, Central America

Provides EMC services for:
automobiles, accessories or parts.

Prestige U.S. Exports
P. O. Box 1493
Bradenton, FL 34206

Phone: (813) 745-5013
Fax: (813) 746-7387

Contact: Leo A. Maka, President
Year Established: 1987

Foreign language capabilities: All Latin origins
Geographic specialization: Worldwide

Provides EMC services for:
air and water purification, pollution control and environmental control products and equipment; audio-visual equipment and educational/training aids; building materials; chemicals, chemical and petrochemical industries equipment and products; computers, peripherals, business equipment and software; electrical, radio and TV, equipment and parts; heating, air-conditioning and refrigeration; industrial products and equipment; medical equipment; materials handling equipment. Handles all products and functions as a brokerage.

Quatro International, Inc.
14147 S.W. 142nd Ave.
Miami, FL 33116-5656

Phone: (305) 233-9580
Fax: (305) 252-1501

Contact: Diego D. Ayala, President
Year Established: 1987

Foreign language capabilities: Spanish
Geographic specialization: Central & South America

Provides EMC services for:
aircraft, accessories or parts; apparel, textiles, garment components and leather goods; building materials; communication equipment and systems; construction equipment; household furnishings and appliances; lighting; medical equipment; pharmaceuticals and hospital supplies; public utilities; restaurant, hotel and catering equipment; safety and security equipment; time recorders and systems.

Rexton Corp.
1700 N.W. 93rd Ave.
Miami, FL 33172

Phone: (305) 592-6085
Fax: (305) 592-7516
Telex 317267

Foreign language capabilities: Spanish

Provides EMC services for:
automobiles, accessories or parts.

San Pedro Products, Co.
P. O. Box 4279
St. Agustine, FL 32085

Phone: (904) 829-6778
Fax: (904) 829-0328

Contact: Arthur J. Ocuto, President
Year Established: 1985

Foreign language capabilities: Spanish
Geographic specialization: Latin America, Caribbean

Provides EMC services for:
automobiles, accessories or parts; farm equipment and products; gasolines, lubricants, and equipment; hardware; heating, air-conditioning and refrigeration; industrial products and equipment; machinery and supplies; materials handling equipment; mining equipment, minerals and raw materials; trucks, accessories or parts.

Semsco International
9501 E. Hillsborough Ave.
Tampa, FL 33610

Phone: (813) 620-1557
Fax: (813) 620-4522
Telex 803765 SEMUNINTEL

Contact: M. E. Brown, General Manager
Year Established: 1968

Foreign language capabilities: Spanish
Geographic specialization: Worldwide

Provides EMC services for:
air and water purification, pollution control and environmental control products and equipment; chemicals, chemical and petrochemical industries equipment and products; hardware; industrial products and equipment; machinery and supplies; pipes; valves; fittings; pumps; compressors; distillation and chlorination equipment.

Skyex Inc.
7943 S.W. 3rd St.
North Lauderdale, FL 33068

Phone: (305) 720-0627
Fax: (305) 753-5198

Contact: Julius L. Kluger, Vice President
Year Established: 1987

Foreign language capabilities: Hungarian, German, Yugoslavian
Geographic specialization: Hungary, Austria, Eastern Europe

Provides EMC services for:
automobiles, accessories or parts; communication equipment and systems; computers, peripherals, business equipment and software; electrical, radio and TV, equipment and parts; medical equipment; safety and security equipment.

Zuniga International
14615 S.W. 49th St.
Miami, FL 33175

Phone: (305) 220-5900
Fax: (305) 220-5901

Contact: Julio Zuniga, President

Foreign language capabilities: Spanish
Geographic specialization: Latin America

Provides EMC services for:
automobiles, accessories or parts; chemicals, chemical and petrochemical industries equipment and products; gasolines, lubricants and equipment.

Atali-Mare, Ltd.
1850 Parkway Place, Suite 620
Atlanta, GA 30067
Phone: (404) 427-5803

Contact: Jeffrey Mucci, Vice President
Year Established: 1989

Foreign language capabilities: German, Spanish
Geographic specialization: Latin America, Europe, Asia

Provides EMC services for:
graphic arts, printing equipment and supplies; medical equipment; pharmaceuticals and hospital supplies.

Chihade International, Inc.
3960 Redan Road
Stone Mountain, GA 30083

Phone: (404) 292-5033
Fax: (404) 297-8920
Telex 804296 CHIHADE
Cables: CHIHADE

Contact: Tawfig Y. Chihade, President
Year Established: 1979

Foreign language capabilities: Arabic
Geographic specialization: Middle East

Provides EMC services for:
computers, peripherals, business equipment and software; food processing/packaging machinery and equipment; food products and beverages; household furnishings and appliances; pharmaceuticals and hospital supplies; restaurant, hotel and catering equipment.

Expotech

P. O. Box 920542
Norcross, GA 30092

Phone: (404) 447-6733
Fax: (404) 279-1188

Contact: L. Ernesto Espinel, President

Year Established: 1989

Geographic specialization: Worldwide

Provides EMC services for:
accessories, luggage and jewelry; automobiles, accessories or parts; building materials; computers, peripherals, business equipment and software; consumer service industries: specialized machinery and equipment; farm equipment and products; food processing/packaging machinery and equipment; gasolines, lubricants, and equipment; hardware; machinery and supplies; medical equipment; mining equipment, minerals and raw materials.

Multimart Corporation

P. O. Box 56666
Atlanta, GA 30343

Phone: (404) 525-2727
Fax: (404) 525-9048
Telex 543708 WMP LAW ATL

Contact: John C. Wilson, President
Year Established: 1975

Foreign language capabilities: Spanish, Portuguese, French, German
Geographic specialization: Latin America, Caribbean, Middle East, Far East

Provides EMC services for:
safety and security equipment.

Sosin International, Inc.

1954 Airport Road, Suite 233-B
Atlanta, GA 30341

Phone: (404) 455-1029
Fax: (404) 455-1021
Telex 6502412733 MCI UW

Contact: Frank H. Sosin, President

Year Established: 1985

Foreign language capabilities: Spanish

Provides EMC services for:
aircraft, accessories or parts.

TechBridge Marketing

1270 Knollwood Court
Roswell, GA 30075

Phone: *(404) 594-7255*
Fax: (404) 594-7263

Contact: Malcolm McPherson, President
Year Established: 1988

Foreign language capabilities: French, German
Geographic specialization: Europe, Scandanavia

Provides EMC services for:
computers, peripherals, business equipment and software.

Universal Data Consultants, Inc.
6621 Bay Circle, Suite 210
Norcross, GA 30071

Phone: (404) 446-6733
Fax: (404) 662-8350

Contact: Tammy R. McDaniel, Int'l Manager
Year Established: 1984

Foreign language capabilities: German, French, Spanish
Geographic specialization: Europe, Africa, Asia

Provides EMC services for:
communication equipment and systems; computers, peripherals, business equipment and software; graphic arts, printing equipment and supplies; hardware.

Quest International
521 Ala Moana Blvd., Suite 216
Honolulu, HI 96813

Phone: (808) 521-1379
Fax: (808) 536-9524

Contact: Richard Lim, President
Year Established: 1979

Foreign language capabilities: Chinese, Japanese, German
Geographic specialization: Asia, Pacific Region

Provides EMC services for:
audio-visual equipment and educational/training aids; automobiles, accessories or parts; consumer service industries: specialized machinery and equipment; electrical, radio and TV, equipment and parts; food products and beverages; games, toys, etc.; medical equipment; marine and related products; pharmaceuticals and hospital supplies; safety and security equipment; sporting goods; consumer products. Also provides consulting services.

Timcorp Int'l Marketing Co., Ltd.
615 Piikoi St., Suite 2009
Honolulu, HI 96814

Phone: (808) 536-6223
Fax: (808) 536-6411
Telex 910 240 6405

Contact: R. Dennis Makepeace, President
Year Established: 1987

Foreign language capabilities: Greek, French, Mandarin, Cantonese, Shanghainese, Indonesian, Spanish
Geographic specialization: Asia/Pacific, Latin America, Western & Eastern Europe

Provides EMC services for:
aircraft, accessories or parts; chemicals, chemical and petrochemical industries equipment and products; food processing/packaging machinery and equipment; industrial products and equipment; machinery and supplies; materials handling equipment; paper, packaging and containers; testing equipment.

Tradelink, Inc.
P. O. Box 3701
Boise, ID 83703

Phone: (208) 378-1548
Fax: (208) 375-6563

Contact: Joseph E. Thomas, President
Year Established: 1989

Foreign language capabilities: Japanese
Geographic specialization: Japan

Provides EMC services for:
computers, peripherals, business equipment and software; electrical, radio and TV, equipment and parts; food products and beverages; industrial products and equipment; medical equipment; pharmaceuticals and hospital supplies; sporting goods.

C.C.I., Inc.
1571 Sherman Ave. Annex
Evanston, IL 60201

Phone: (708) 328-7711
Fax: (708) 328-7751

Contact: Richard Lovell, President
Year Established: 1985

Foreign language capabilities: Spanish, French,
German, Japanese, Arabic
Geographic specialization: Worldwide

Provides EMC services for:
aircraft, accessories or parts; automobiles,
accessories or parts; marine and related products;
trucks, accessories or parts; motorcycles.

SEE ADVERTISEMENT, PAGE 37.

Chicago Midwest Export Marketing Corp.
1719 S. Clinton St.
Chicago, IL 60616

Phone: (312) 922-7700
Fax: (312) 421-1109

Contact: George J. Ferguson, President
Year Established: 1980

Foreign language capabilities: Chinese, Spanish
Geographic specialization: China, Latin America,
Africa, Eastern Europe

Provides EMC services for:
farm equipment and products; food
processing/packaging machinery and equipment;
food products and beverages; medical equipment;
mining equipment, minerals and raw materials;
animal feed.

Da Miano & Graham Ltd.
P. O. Box 89
Glenview, IL 60025

Phone: (312) 694-5450
Fax: (708) 635-0916
Telex 275126
Cables: DAGRAM

Contact: Andrew S. Da Miano, President
Year Established: 1953

Foreign language capabilities: Arabic, French,
Spanish, German
Geographic specialization: Worldwide, especially
Middle East

Provides EMC services for:
automobiles, accessories or parts; safety and
security equipment; testing equipment; garage
equipment.

Daretel Group, Inc., The
B-8015 Suite 190
St. Charles, IL 60174

Phone: (708) 365-5601
Fax: (708) 365-5634

Contact: David G. Detert, Chairman

Year Established: 1988
Geographic specialization: Europe

Provides EMC services for:
communication equipment and systems.

Engineering Equipment Co.
1020 W. 31st St.
Downers Grove, IL 60515-0790

Phone: (708) 963-7800
Fax: (708) 963-7123
Telex 253817
Cables: PANMAKINA

Contact: Frank J. Cullen, Vice President
Year Established: 1940

Foreign language capabilities: Spanish
Geographic specialization: Worldwide

Provides EMC services for:
air and water purification, pollution control and environmental control products and equipment; automobiles, accessories or parts; construction equipment; industrial products and equipment; machinery and supplies; materials handling equipment; public utilities; safety and security equipment; trucks, accessories or parts; fire fighting equipment; cranes and draglines; weighing and road building equipment; asphalt and concrete batching plants.

EX-IM U.S.A., Inc.
1000 Tower Lane, Suite 175
Bensenville, IL 60106

Phone: (708) 595-0003
Fax: (708) 595-7001

Contact: Inkuk Chung, Managing Director
Year Established: 1987

Foreign language capabilities: Japanese, Korean, Chinese
Geographic specialization: Far East

Provides EMC services for:
accessories, luggage and jewelry; automobiles, accessories or parts; building materials; consumer service industries: specialized machinery and equipment; food processing/packaging machinery and equipment; industrial products and equipment; machinery and supplies; marine and related products; sporting goods. Performs import-export functions.

ERW International Inc.
P. O. Box 690-L
Barrington, IL 60011

Phone: (703) 381-7972
Fax: (708) 381-5892
Telex 754355 ERW/SYNAB
Cables: INTERERG

Contact: Kathy Umlauf, President
Year Established: 1976

Provides EMC services for:
automobiles, accessories or parts; graphic arts, printing equipment and supplies; medical equipment; materials handling equipment; pharmaceuticals and hospital supplies; safety and security equipment; trucks, accessories or parts. Also provides consulting services.

Fields International
201 N. Wells St.
Chicago, IL 60606

Phone: (312) 726-6126
Fax: (312) 726-7512
Telex 6871014 FIELD UW
Cables: INTERFIELD

Contact: Sydney M. Fields, President
Year Established: 1955

Foreign language capabilities: Spanish, French, Italian, German
Geographic specialization: Worldwide

Provides EMC services for:
automobiles, accessories or parts; building materials; construction equipment; hardware; industrial products and equipment; machinery and supplies; materials handling equipment; restaurant, hotel and catering equipment; trucks, accessories or parts. Also provides consulting services.

FWD International, Inc.
1020 W. 31st St.
Downers Grove, IL 60515

Phone: (708) 963-7800
Fax: (708) 963-7123
Telex 253817

Contact: Frank J. Cullen, Vice President
Year Established: 1951

Foreign language capabilities: Spanish
Geographic specialization: Worldwide, except North America

Provides EMC services for:
construction equipment; mining equipment, minerals and raw materials; trucks, accessories or parts; heavy duty off-highway vehicles.

Honigberg, J. D., Int'l, Inc.
5737 W. Howard St.
Chicago, IL 60648

Phone: (708) 647-6828
Fax: (708) 647-7126
Telex 4932099 JDH INTL

Contact: Albert Elkaim, Export Director
Year Established: 1980

Foreign language capabilities: German, Italian, Spanish, French, some Japanese
Geographic specialization: Europe, Far East, Australia, Pacific Rim

Provides EMC services for:
medical equipment; restaurant, hotel and catering equipment; irrigation equipment.

Industrial Engineering Int'l, Inc.
1701 W. Quincy Ave., No. 3
Naperville, IL 60540

Phone: (708) 355-8770
Fax: (708) 355-8791
Telex 386124 IEI INC

Contact: John G. Penalosa M., President

Geographic specialization: Worldwide

Provides EMC services for:
automobiles, accessories or parts; industrial products and equipment.

International Marketing Consultants Inc.
17 W. 755 Butterfield Rd.
Oakbrook Terrace, IL 60181

Phone: (708) 932-0033
Fax: (708) 932-0908
Telex 401658 IMC INC

Contact: Morteza Setayesh, Director, International Sales
Year Established: 1985

Foreign language capabilities: Spanish, French
Geographic specialization: Worldwide

Provides EMC services for:
construction equipment; farm equipment and products; hardware; heating, air-conditioning and refrigeration; household furnishings and appliances; machinery and supplies; sporting goods; testing equipment; lawn and garden products; lawnmowers.

J & M Company, Ltd.
655 Plum Tree Road
Barrington Hills, IL 60010

Phone: (708) 639-1555
Fax: (708) 639-8710

Contact: James P. Antonic, President
Year Established: 1980

Foreign language capabilities: Japanese, French, German, Spanish
Geographic specialization: Japan, Pacific Rim

Provides EMC services for:
automobiles, accessories or parts; building materials; chemicals, chemical and petrochemical industries equipment and products; furniture; hardware; household furnishings and appliances; industrial products and equipment; lighting; sporting goods; compressed air accessories.

Kammeh Int'l Trade Co.
1718 N. Sayre Ave.
Chicago, IL 60635-4323

Phone: (312) 804-0800
Fax: (312) 804-0804
Cables: KAMM

Contact: Dr. Reza Rezai, President
Year Established: 1987

Foreign language capabilities: French, Spanish, German, Italian, Farsi, Japanese, Hebrew, Kurdish
Geographic specialization: Europe, Far East, South America

Provides EMC services for:
accessories, luggage and jewelry; air and water purification, pollution control and environmental control products and equipment; apparel, textiles, garment components and leather goods; building materials; chemicals, chemical and petrochemical industries equipment and products; computers, peripherals, business equipment and software; consumer service industries: specialized machinery and equipment; furniture; optical, photographic, and scientific instruments; paper, packaging and containers; restaurant, hotel and catering equipment; sporting goods; trucks, accessories or parts; general merchandise.

Kellogg International, Inc.
421 Wilkins Dr.
Des Plaines, IL 60016

Phone: (708) 299-7629
Fax: (708) 390-9889
Telex 984063 GARBAREK CGO

Contact: Lawrence E. Garbarek, General Manager
Year Established: 1984

Foreign language capabilities: Spanish, Korean
Geographic specialization: Worldwide, except North America

Provides EMC services for:
aircraft, accessories or parts; industrial products and equipment; machinery and supplies.

LKS International
4001 W. Devon Ave.
Chicago, IL 60646

Phone: (312) 283-6601
Fax: (312) 283-6710
Telex 853317

Contact: Walter P. Lehmann, President
Year Established: 1984

Foreign language capabilities: Spanish, German, French, Swiss, Russian, Polish
Geographic specialization: Worldwide

Provides EMC services for:
automobiles, accessories or parts; restaurant, hotel and catering equipment.

Medica International, Ltd.

360 N. Michigan Ave., Suite 2001
Chicago, IL 60601-3805

Phone: (312) 263-1117
Fax: (312) 263-1036
Telex 25-3618
Cables: "MEDICAINT", CHICAGO

Contact: James M. Davran, Vice President
Year Established: 1954

Foreign language capabilities: Spanish, French, Portuguese, Italian, German, Greek, Tagalog
Geographic specialization: Asia, Australia, Middle East, Latin America, Canada, Western Europe

Provides EMC services for:
farm equipment and products; heating, air-conditioning and refrigeration; medical equipment; pharmaceuticals and hospital supplies; restaurant, hotel and catering equipment; agricultural chemicals and fertilizers.

Midwestern Trading Corp.

P. O. Box 243
Oak Forest, IL 60452

Phone: (708) 687-8410
Fax: (708) 687-2865
Cables: MIDWESTCO

Contact: Sean Carrera, General Manager
Year Established: 1973

Foreign language capabilities: Russian, Italian, French, Japanese, Spanish, German
Geographic specialization: Southeast Asia, Europe, Brazil, Mexico, Canada

Provides EMC services for:
accessories, luggage and jewelry; aircraft, accessories or parts; audio-visual equipment and educational/training aids; building materials; construction equipment; electrical, radio and TV, equipment and parts; furniture; household furnishings and appliances; industrial products and equipment; optical, photographic, and scientific instruments; testing equipment; trucks, accessories or parts; specialties are electomagnetic shieldings and specialty coatings; cosmetics. Handles all types of products.

Neslo International Ltd.

P. O. Box 231
Mount Prospect, IL 60056

Phone: (708) 437-4224
Fax: (708) 437-4231
Cables: NORDUFFO

Contact: Norman D. Olsen, President
Year Established: 1956

Foreign language capabilities: Spanish
Geographic specialization: Worldwide

Provides EMC services for:
farm equipment and products; dairy farm and veterinarian supplies.

Overseas Services Corp.

1230 W. Northwest Highway
Palatine, IL 60067

Phone: (708) 934-3883
Fax: (708) 381-0766

Contact: Mark Sageser, President
Year Established: 1989

Foreign language capabilities: German, Spanish
Geographic specialization: Worldwide

Provides EMC services for:
air and water purification, pollution control and environmental control products and equipment; building materials; food processing/packaging machinery and equipment. Also provides consulting services.

PNR International, Ltd.

1435 Joyce Avenue
Palatine, IL 60067

Phone: (708) 934-1705
Fax: (708) 934-8118

Contact: Peter Salter, President
Year Established: 1986

Foreign language capabilities: German, Spanish
Geographic specialization: Worldwide

Provides EMC services for:
chemicals, chemical and petrochemical industries equipment and products; computers, peripherals, business equipment and software; heating, air-conditioning and refrigeration; machinery and supplies; materials handling equipment; testing equipment; metal-working machinery; pipeline maintenance equipment.

RKF International Inc.

225 No. Michigan Ave., Suite 1226
Chicago, IL 60601

Phone: (312) 616-0012
Fax: (312) 616-0018

Contact: Robert K. Foley, President
Year Established: 1987

Foreign language capabilities: Most foreign languages
Geographic specialization: North & South America, Asia, Europe

Provides EMC services for:
air and water purification, pollution control and environmental control products and equipment; aircraft, accessories or parts; apparel, textiles, garment components and leather goods; audio-visual equipment and educational/training aids; chemicals, chemical and petrochemical industries equipment and products; games, toys, etc.; graphic arts, printing equipment and supplies; hardware; heating, air-conditioning and refrigeration; household furnishings and appliances; safety and security equipment; sporting goods.

EMCs & CONSULTANTS

If your company is not listed in the

DIRECTORY OF LEADING U.S. EXPORT MANAGEMENT COMPANIES

and you would like to be included in the next edition,
contact Bergano Book Co. for a free listing application.

Bergano Book Co.
P.O. Box 190
Fairfield, CT 06430

Phone: (203) 254-2054

Robco International Corporation

P. O. Box 707
Oak Park, IL 60303

Phone: (708) 524-1880
Fax: (708) 524-2015
Telex 210045 INTSER-UR
Cables: ROBCO CHICAGO

Contact: Robert F. Begani, President
Year Established: 1976

Foreign language capabilities: Spanish, French
Geographic specialization: Worldwide

Provides EMC services for:
automobiles, accessories or parts; building materials; chemicals, chemical and petrochemical industries equipment and products; farm equipment and products; heating, air-conditioning and refrigeration; industrial products and equipment.

Subent Co., Inc.

1 S. 376 Summit Ave., Suite 6F
Oakbrook Terrace, IL 60181

Phone: (708) 953-1600
Fax: (708) 691-1406
Telex 72-1473

Contact: George Lacina, President

Year Established: 1960

Geographic specialization: Worldwide

Provides EMC services for:
air and water purification, pollution control and environmental control products and equipment; lighting.

Aztek International Corp.

P. O. Box 11409
Ft. Wayne, IN 46858-1409

Phone: (219) 747-4201
Fax: (219) 747-7306
Cables: AZTEK-FORT WAYNE

Contact: Stanley J. Stevens, President
Year Established: 1980

Foreign language capabilities: Spanish, French, Greek, Italian, Portuguese
Geographic specialization: Worldwide

Provides EMC services for:
accessories, luggage and jewelry; air and water purification, pollution control and environmental control products and equipment; automobiles, accessories or parts; consumer service industries: specialized machinery and equipment; farm equipment and products; food processing/ packaging machinery and equipment; games, toys, etc.; hardware; household furnishings and appliances; industrial products and equipment; materials handling equipment.

Curtis TradeGroup, Inc.

1000 Waterway Blvd.
Indianapolis, IN 46202

Phone: (317) 633-2048
Fax: (317) 634-1791
Telex 27440 (CURTIS USA)

Contact: James M. Haberman, President
Year Established: 1990

Foreign language capabilities: French
Geographic specialization: Worldwide

Provides EMC services for:
chemicals, chemical and petrochemical industries equipment and products; electrical, radio and TV, equipment and parts; industrial products and equipment; medical equipment; scrap rubber; vinyl inflatables.

Export Agencies Int'l Corp.

P. O. Box 900
Fort Wayne, IN 46801

Phone: (219) 747-7876
Fax: (219) 747-6555
Telex 798829
Cables: EXAGEN - FT. WAYNE

Contact: J. H. Osborne, Vice President
Year Established: 1929

Foreign language capabilities: Spanish, French, German
Geographic specialization: Worldwide

Provides EMC services for:
automobiles, accessories or parts.

Geon International Corp.

P. O. Box 1000
Fort Wayne, IN 46801

Phone: (219) 747-6863
Fax: (219) 747-6555
Telex 988426
Cables: GEON/FT. WAYNE

Contact: E. F. Grossman, Vice President
Year Established: 1946

Foreign language capabilities: Spanish, French, German
Geographic specialization: Worldwide

Provides EMC services for:
automobiles, accessories or parts; trucks, accessories or parts.

Gerson International Corp.

P. O. Box 565
Fort Wayne, IN 46801

Phone: (219) 747-3141
Fax: (219) 747-6555
Telex 232482
Cables: GERSON-FT. WAYNE

Contact: J. R. Gerson, President
Year Established: 1964

Foreign language capabilities: Spanish, French, German
Geographic specialization: Worldwide

Provides EMC services for:
automobiles, accessories or parts.

Nagro-Berry International

221 N. Main St., Suite 220
Goshen, IN 46526

Phone: (219) 534-5822
Fax: (219) 534-5922

Contact: Phillip R. Berry, President
Year Established: 1988

Foreign language capabilities: Japanese
Geographic specialization: Pacific Rim, Japan

Provides EMC services for:
heating, air-conditioning and refrigeration; industrial products and equipment; machinery and supplies; paper, packaging and containers; testing equipment; recreational vehicles; playground equipment.

Schwanke Int'l Marketing Corp.

P. O. Box 1050
South Bend, IN 46624

Phone: (219) 259-1966
Fax: (219) 259-6846
Telex 258-447 SIMCORP MIKA
Cables: SIMCORP

Contact: F. R. Schwanke, President

Year Established: 1971

Geographic specialization: Worldwide

Provides EMC services for:
automobiles, accessories or parts; food products and beverages; medical equipment; trucks, accessories or parts.

United Export Corporation

P. O. Box 147
South Bend, IN 46624

Phone: (219) 232-8286
Fax: (219) 232-8295
Telex 6731228UNITEDUW

Contact: Peter F. Baranay, President
Year Established: 1939

Foreign language capabilities: Spanish, French, Japanese
Geographic specialization: Worldwide, especially developing countries

Provides EMC services for:
automobiles, accessories or parts; hardware; heating, air-conditioning and refrigeration; industrial products and equipment; safety and security equipment; sporting goods.

AEON International Corp.

360 Seventh Ave.
Marion, IA 52302

Phone: (319) 377-7415
Fax: (319) 377-6514
Telex 439071
Cables: AEON

Contact: C. M. Adams, President
Year Established: 1946

Foreign language capabilities: Spanish
Geographic specialization: Worldwide

Provides EMC services for:
farm equipment and products; furniture; materials handling equipment; office furniture. Performs export trading company services.

Dunlap International

P. O. Box 1802
Cedar Rapids, IA 52406

Phone: (319) 366-7732
Fax: (319) 377-5667
Telex 510-601-2507 BEXCO INTL UQ

Contact: Karen Dunlap, President
Year Established: 1989

Foreign language capabilities: Spanish
Geographic specialization: Worldwide

Provides EMC services for:
chemicals, chemical and petrochemical industries equipment and products; farm equipment and products; food processing/packaging machinery and equipment; lighting; medical equipment; materials handling equipment; paper, packaging and containers; pharmaceuticals and hospital supplies; restaurant, hotel and catering equipment; sporting goods; trucks, accessories or parts. Provides export trading company services.

Iowa Export Import Trading Co.

601 Locust St, Suite 200G
Des Moines, IA 50309

Phone: (515) 245-2464
Fax: (515) 282-1038

Contact: David Peterson, Product Manager
Year Established: 1983

Foreign language capabilities: German, Spanish
Geographic specialization: Worldwide

Provides EMC services for:
automobiles, accessories or parts; farm equipment and products; trucks, accessories or parts.

United Exporters Service, Inc.

708 Brightwood Place, Suite A-2
Louisville, KY 40207

Phone: (502) 893-8661
Fax: (502) 893-3918

Contact: Charles H. Chang, President
Year Established: 1989

Foreign language capabilities: Chinese, German
Geographic specialization: Asia, UK, Europe & Africa

Provides EMC services for:
air and water purification, pollution control and environmental control products and equipment; automobiles, accessories or parts; building materials; electrical, radio and TV, equipment and parts; farm equipment and products; food processing/packaging machinery and equipment; food products and beverages; heating, A/C and refrigeration; medical equipment; pharmaceuticals and hospital supplies; safety and security equipment; Arabian, Kentucky thoroughbred horses. Also provides consulting services.

Fairco, Inc.

518 Gravier St.
New Orleans, LA 70130

Phone: (504) 524-0467
Fax: (504) 524-6931
Telex 6821206

Contact: Edgar C. Bourg, Vice President
Year Established: 1946

Foreign language capabilities: Spanish, French, German
Geographic specialization: Worldwide

Provides EMC services for:
food products and beverages.

Gibbons, J.T., Inc.

P. O. Box 50579
New Orleans, LA 70150

Phone: (504) 831-9907
Fax: (504) 837-5516
Telex 6821115-JTGC UW

Contact: Tony Jarana, Sales Manager
Year Established: 1862

Foreign language capabilities: Spanish, French, Arabic
Geographic specialization: Middle East, Caribbean, Central America

Provides EMC services for:
food products and beverages; household products, toiletries and cosmetics.

Inter-America Sales Co., Inc.
2207 Kingston St.
Kenner, LA 70062

Phone: (504) 464-6162
Fax: (504) 464-6179

Contact: Louis E. Perez, Jr. President
Year Established: 1955

Foreign language capabilities: English, Spanish
Geographic specialization: Latin America,
Western Hemisphere

Provides EMC services for:
food processing/packaging machinery and
equipment; heating, air-conditioning and
refrigeration; restaurant, hotel and catering
equipment; energy management systems.

Electrical Manufacturers Export Co.
P. O. Box 641
Castine, ME 04421
Phone: (207) 326-9472
Cables: BERLAGE, CASTINE

Contact: Fred van der Togt, Export Manager
Year Established: 1919

Foreign language capabilities: English, Dutch,
French, German, Spanish
Geographic specialization: Worldwide

Provides EMC services for:
chemicals, chemical and petrochemical industries
equipment and products; electrical, radio and TV,
equipment and parts; medical equipment.

Moran's International Services
3 Hanson Dr.
Topsham, ME 04086

Phone: (207) 729-2709
Fax: (207) 729-8609

Contact: Robert B. Moran, President
Year Established: 1989

Foreign language capabilities: Spanish
Geographic specialization: Europe, Asia

Provides EMC services for:
sporting goods.

Protrade International
20 West St., Suite 31
Portland, ME 04102

Phone: (207) 879-1922
Fax: (207) 773-2428
Telex 4933966 PROTRADE

Contact: Angus L. Garfield, President
Year Established: 1987

Foreign language capabilities: French
Geographic specialization: Europe, Middle East,
Canada

Provides EMC services for:
automobiles, accessories or parts; building
materials; construction equipment; furniture;
hardware; household furnishings and appliances;
machinery and supplies; medical equipment;
materials handling equipment; mining equipment,
minerals and raw materials; pharmaceuticals and
hospital supplies; restaurant, hotel and catering
equipment; sporting goods; energy-saving
showerheads.

Dosik International
9519 Evergreen St.
Silver Springs, MD 20901
Phone: (301) 585-4259

Contact: Stanely Dosik, President
Year Established: 1982

Foreign language capabilities: German, Italian
Geographic specialization: Worldwide

Provides EMC services for:
medical equipment; optical, photographic, and
scientific instruments.

Exportus Ltd.
831 Glen Allen Drive
Baltimore, MD 21229

Phone: (301) 947-0644
Fax: (301) 744-9409
Telex 981-292

Contact: Timothy S. McKinnon, Vice President
Year Established: 1988

Foreign language capabilities: Spanish
Geographic specialization: Latin America, South
America, Caribbean, Africa

Provides EMC services for:
safety and security equipment.

INEX Technology International
15954 Derwood Rd.
Rockville, MD 20855

Phone: (301) 330-9664
Fax: (301) 762-0562

Contact: John M. Stout, President

Year Established: 1988

Geographic specialization: Western & Eastern
Europe, Asia/Pacific, China, Africa

Provides EMC services for:
communication equipment and systems;
computers, peripherals, business equipment and
software.

International Purchasers
25 Main St., Suite 202
Reisterstown, MD 21136

Phone: (301) 833-6400
Fax: (301) 833-3429
Telex 198132
Cables: INTLPURCH REIS

Contact: William J. Gisiner, Jr., President
Year Established: 1974

Foreign language capabilities: Spanish
Geographic specialization: Central & South
America

Provides EMC services for:
chemicals, chemical and petrochemical industries
equipment and products; construction equipment;
industrial products and equipment; machinery and
supplies; materials handling equipment; mining
equipment, minerals and raw materials. Also
performs export trading company services.

Rajiv International, Inc.
8000 Philadelphia Road
Baltimore, MD 21237

Phone: (301) 477-6179
Fax: (301) 683-1319
Telex 151280384

Contact: Brian R. Lazarus, President
Year Established: 1983

Foreign language capabilities: German, Spanish
Geographic specialization: Worldwide, especially
developing countries

Provides EMC services for:
air and water purification, pollution control and
environmental control products and equipment;
building materials; food processing/packaging
machinery and equipment; food products and
beverages; medical equipment.

Spivey, James S., Inc.
P. O. Box 175
Kensington, MD 20895

Phone: (301) 656-6028
Fax: (301) 656-6433
Telex 898388 AEMPWR WASH
Cables: JASPIVE BETHESDA, MD.

Contact: James S. Spivey, President
Year Established: 1946

Foreign language capabilities: Spanish
Geographic specialization: Worldwide

Provides EMC services for:
aircraft, accessories or parts; communication
equipment and systems; trucks, accessories or
parts; military personnel equipment.

American Eagle Purchasing Agents, Inc.
P. O. Box 3423 McCormack Station
Boston, MA 02101

Phone: (617) 846-6630
Fax: (617) 846-3406
Telex 174365 AMEAGLE
Cables: "AMEAGLE-MA"

Contact: Gregory F. Tzannos, Export Manager

Year Established: 1987

Geographic specialization: Worldwide

Provides EMC services for:
air and water purification, pollution control and
environmental control products and equipment;
communication equipment and systems. Also
functions as purchasing agents.

AmTech Organization Inc.
232 Tosca Drive
Stoughton, MA 02072

Phone: (617) 344-1550
Fax: (617) 344-1992

Contact: Stephen C. Spector, President
Year Established: 1988

Foreign language capabilities: Spanish, French,
German
Geographic specialization: Worldwide

Provides EMC services for:
computers, peripherals, business equipment and
software.

ARC International Group, Inc.
111 Boston Post Road
Sudbury, MA 01776

Phone: (508) 443-1820
Fax: (508) 443-1898

Contact: Robert C. V. Chen, President
Year Established: 1988

Foreign language capabilities: Chinese, Thai, Spanish, Korean
Geographic specialization: Pacific Rim, South America

Provides EMC services for:
air and water purification, pollution control and environmental control products and equipment; apparel, textiles, garment components and leather goods; building materials; chemicals, chemical and petrochemical industries equipment and products; communication equipment and systems; computers, peripherals, business equipment and software; construction equipment; electrical, radio and TV, equipment and parts; farm equipment and products; graphic arts, printing equipment and supplies; hardware; industrial products and equipment; medical equipment; pharmaceuticals and hospital supplies; safety and security equip.

Chemical Export Company, Inc.
262 Washington St.
Boston, MA 02108

Phone: (617) 742-1661
Fax: (617) 742-2217
Telex 203508 CHEMCO BSN

Contact: Herbert Kimiatek, President
Year Established: 1946

Foreign language capabilities: Spanish, French, Hungarian, Slovak
Geographic specialization: Latin America, Far East

Provides EMC services for:
chemicals, chemical and petrochemical industries equipment and products; industrial products and equipment; paints, varnishes and enamels; pharmaceuticals and hospital supplies.

Cobble Hill International
Box 204 Mathews Road
Conway, MA 01373

Phone: (413) 625-8422
Fax: (413) 665-8688

Contact: J. David Magagna, President
Year Established: 1972

Foreign language capabilities: Japanese, Chinese, German, Italian
Geographic specialization: Europe, Far East

Provides EMC services for:
communication equipment and systems; computers, peripherals, business equipment and software; electrical, radio and TV, equipment and parts; food products and beverages; medical equipment; optical, photographic, and scientific instruments; sporting goods; testing equipment; musical instruments.

Crown Automotive Sales Co., Inc.
340 Oak Street
No. Pembroke, MA 02358

Phone: (617) 826-6200
Fax: (617) 826-4097
Telex 921852

Contact: Herbert J. Gerber, President

Provides EMC services for:
automobiles, accessories or parts.

Glynn International, Inc.

14 Alton Court
Brookline, MA 02146

Phone: (617) 232-5400
Fax: (617) 734-0271

Contact: D. Keveny, Managing Director
Year Established: 1986

Foreign language capabilities: Most languages offered
Geographic specialization: Western & Eastern Europe, Far East

Provides EMC services for:
air and water purification, pollution control and environmental control products and equip.; audio-visual equipment and educational/training aids; building materials; chemicals, chemical and petro-chemical industries equipment and products; communication equipment and systems; computers, peripherals, business equip. and software; construc-tion equipment; consumer service industries: specialized machinery and equipment; food processing/ packaging machinery and equipment; industrial products and equipment; medical equip.; pharmaceuticals and hospital supplies; testing equipment. Also provides consulting services.

Intrax

30 Colpitts Rd.
Weston, MA 02193

Phone: (617) 893-3111
Fax: (617) 899-8726

Contact: Thomas A. Blatt, President
Year Established: 1975

Foreign language capabilities: Italian, Hungarian, French
Geographic specialization: Western & Eastern Europe

Provides EMC services for:
communication equipment and systems; industrial products and equipment; machinery and supplies; medical equipment; optical, photographic, and scientific instruments; safety and security equipment; testing equipment.

McKim Group

225 Riverview Ave.
Waltham, MA 02254

Phone: (617) 647-5560
Fax: (617) 891-8375
Telex RCA 200182 MCKIM UR
Cables: MCKIM-BOSTON

Contact: Joe Pires, Vice President
Year Established: 1925

Foreign language capabilities: Portuguese, Spanish, French
Geographic specialization: Worldwide, except Canada

Provides EMC services for:
building materials; chemicals, chemical and petrochemical industries equipment and products; construction equipment; electrical, radio and TV, equipment and parts; farm equipment and products; hardware; industrial products and equipment; materials handling equipment; lawn and garden tools.

Reed, Charles H. Export, Inc.

734 Main St.
Norwell, MA 02061

Phone: (617) 659-1555
Fax: (617) 659-1357

Contact: Damon P. Reed, President
Year Established: 1950

Foreign language capabilities: Spanish
Geographic specialization: Worldwide

Provides EMC services for:
communication equipment and systems; food processing/packaging machinery and equipment; mining equipment, minerals and raw materials; paper, packaging and containers; sporting goods; public seating for stadiums and sport halls.

Software Export Corp.
P. O. Box 32
Cambridge, MA 02139

Phone: (617) 642-5726
Fax: (617) 642-5726

Contact: Michael Rooney, Chairman
Year Established: 1989

Foreign language capabilities: Many European and Asian languages
Geographic specialization: Europe, Asia, Australia, Japan

Provides EMC services for:
computers, peripherals, business equipment and software.

Surel International, Inc.
6 Country Lane
Medway, MA 02053

Phone: (508) 533-5175
Fax: (508) 533-5582
Telex 710-347-7538

Contact: Emil G. Surel, President
Year Established: 1972

Foreign language capabilities: French
Geographic specialization: Worldwide

Provides EMC services for:
air and water purification, pollution control and environmental control products and equipment; audio-visual equipment and educational/training aids; computers, peripherals, business equipment and software; electrical, radio and TV, equipment and parts; testing equipment; professional electronics.

Wellesley International Corp.
148 Linden St.
Wellesley, MA 02181

Phone: (617) 235-2000
Fax: (617) 239-1616
Telex 4973200 WLSY UI

Contact: William C. Poellmitz, President
Year Established: 1985

Foreign language capabilities: Spanish, German, French, Portuguese, Japanese, Chinese
Geographic specialization: Worldwide

Provides EMC services for:
air and water purification, pollution control and environmental control products and equip.; aircraft, accessories or parts; chemicals, chemical and petrochemical industries equip. and products; communication equip. and systems; electrical, radio and TV, equip. and parts; food processing/packaging machinery and equip.; household furnishings and appliances; industrial products; lighting; machinery and supplies; medical equip.; optical, photographic, and scientific instruments; public utilities; safety and security equip.; sporting goods; time recorders and systems; testing equip. Also has a division handling consulting projects.

ZED Group, Inc.
IMC Box 6475
Chelsea, MA 02150

Phone: (617) 889-2220
Fax: (617) 889-0170

Contact: Robert Zisa, President
Year Established: 1970

Foreign language capabilities: Spanish, Italian, French, German
Geographic specialization: Worldwide

Provides EMC services for:
air and water purification, pollution control and environmental control products and equipment; consumer service industries: specialized machinery and equipment; hardware; industrial products and equipment; lighting; machinery and supplies; optical, photographic, and scientific instruments; tools for hobby and craft work.

Detroit Parts Mfg. Co.

1363 Anderson Road
Clawson, MI 48017

Phone: (313) 435-2550
Fax: (313) 435-3678
Telex ITT 4320059
Cables: DEPARTS

Contact: J. M. Gruen, President

Foreign language capabilities: Spanish
Geographic specialization: Mexico, South
America, Sweden, South Africa

Provides EMC services for:
automobiles, accessories or parts; trucks,
accessories or parts.

Intertrade, Inc.

P. O. Box 706
Franklin, MI 48025

Phone: (313) 851-5810
Fax: (313) 626-6193
Telex 530453 INTERTRADE

Contact: Mr./Mrs. Katz
Year Established: 1984

Foreign language capabilities: Chinese, French
Geographic specialization: Developed countries

Provides EMC services for:
automobiles, accessories or parts; furniture;
household furnishings and appliances; sporting
goods; leisure products.

Intraco Corporation

1410 Allen Drive
Troy, MI 48083-4001

Phone: (313) 585-6900
Fax: (313) 585-6920
Telex 6877118 INTRA UW

Contact: Dan Wywoda, Vice President - Operations
Year Established: 1971

Foreign language capabilities: Arabic, French,
Spanish, German
Geographic specialization: Middle East,
Northern Africa

Provides EMC services for:
automobiles, accessories or parts; building
materials; heating, air-conditioning and
refrigeration; trucks, accessories or parts; drilling
equipment; construction glass; automotive glass.

Kalamazoo International, Inc.

P. O. Box 271
South Haven, MI 49090

Phone: (616) 637-2178
Fax: (616) 637-2275
Telex 729452 (JENJEN SHAV)
Cables: JENJEN

Contact: John C. Jensen, President
Year Established: 1960

Foreign language capabilities: French, Spanish
Geographic specialization: Worldwide

Provides EMC services for:
aircraft, accessories or parts; automobiles,
accessories or parts; chemicals, chemical and
petrochemical industries equipment and products;
farm equipment and products; industrial products
and equipment; paper, packaging and containers;
safety and security equipment.

Robb, R. Int'l Associates, Inc.
8230 Goldie St.
Walled Lake, MI 48088-1298

Phone: (313) 363-6888
Fax: (313) 363-7998
Telex 231238 RICROB SOFD
Cables: RICROB DETROIT

Contact: John D. Gerrard, Vice President, Export

Provides EMC services for:
automobiles, accessories or parts; machinery and supplies.

Amex, Inc.
2724 Summer St., N.E.
Minneapolis, MN 55413

Phone: (612) 331-3063
Fax: (612) 331-3180
Telex 4998367 AMEXI

Contact: Dale West, General Manager
Year Established: 1981

Foreign language capabilities: Spanish, Arabic, French
Geographic specialization: Worldwide

Provides EMC services for:
communication equipment and systems; computers, peripherals, business equipment and software; construction equipment; heating, air-conditioning and refrigeration; industrial products and equipment; machinery and supplies; medical equipment; testing equipment; trucks, accessories or parts; electronics.

Computer Commodities Int'l
7573 Golden Triangle Dr.
Minneapolis, MN 55344

Phone: (612) 942-0992
Fax: (612) 942-8712

Contact: Robert A. Kern, President

Year Established: 1987
Geographic specialization: Eastern & Western Europe, Japan

Provides EMC services for:
computers, peripherals, business equipment and software.

SEE ADVERTISEMENT, PAGE 51.

Trade Management Services
5151 Edina Industrial Blvd., Suite 121
Edina, MN 55439

Phone: (612) 835-1702
Fax: (612) 835-1704

Contact: Thomas H. Kalgren, Vice President
Year Established: 1989

Foreign language capabilities: All languages available
Geographic specialization: Worldwide

Provides EMC services for:
marine and related products; safety and security equipment; sporting goods; fishing- and hunting-related products.

Dynacon
9953 Lewis & Clark Blvd., Suite 208
St. Louis, MO 63136

Phone: (314) 869-4482
Fax: (314) 355-2596
Telex 424089

Contact: Herman Cordoba, President
Year Established: 1980

Foreign language capabilities: Spanish, French, Italian, Portuguese, Korean
Geographic specialization: Latin America, Far East, Europe, Middle East

Provides EMC services for:
building materials; farm equipment and products; industrial products and equipment; medical equipment; mining equipment, minerals and raw materials; pharmaceuticals and hospital supplies; trucks, accessories or parts.

Hosler & Associates, Inc.
P. O. Box 415
Ballwin, MO 63022

Phone: (314) 394-3436
Fax: (314) 527-4608

Contact: James W. Hosler, President

Year Established: 1978
Geographic specialization: South America, Southeast Asia

Provides EMC services for:
automobiles, accessories or parts; consumer service industries: specialized machinery and equipment; industrial products and equipment; lighting; machinery and supplies; electrical transformers.

Roldan Products Corporation
4455 Duncan Ave.
St. Louis, MO 63110

Phone: (314) 652-3737
Fax: (314) 652-9527
Cables: ROLDAN-ST. LOUIS

Contact: Joseph G. Roldan, Chairman
Year Established: 1925

Foreign language capabilities: Spanish
Geographic specialization: Worldwide

Provides EMC services for:
accessories, luggage and jewelry; apparel, textiles, garment components and leather goods; building materials; computers, peripherals, business equipment and software; farm equipment and products; furniture; graphic arts, printing equipment and supplies; household furnishings and appliances; lighting; medical equipment; optical, photographic, and scientific instruments; restaurant, hotel and catering equipment.

Fernandez Import/Export, Inc. USA
P. O. Box 3535
Gastonia, NC 28053

Phone: (704) 867-9999
Fax: (704) 868-8688
Telex 802186

Contact: Tony Fernandez, President
Year Established: 1975

Foreign language capabilities: Malasian, Indonesian
Geographic specialization: Southeast Asia, Yugoslavia

Provides EMC services for:
apparel, textiles, garment components and leather goods; automobiles, accessories or parts; computers, peripherals, business equipment and software; furniture; medical equipment; pharmaceuticals and hospital supplies; restaurant, hotel and catering equipment; safety and security equipment; trucks, accessories or parts.

Global Marketing Concepts

4101 West Blvd.
Charlotte, NC 28219

Phone: (704) 398-2352
Fax: (704) 394-9255
Telex 413540

Contact: Thad Cloer, President
Year Established: 1989

Foreign language capabilities: Many languages available
Geographic specialization: Asia, Central & South America, Mexico, Caribbean, West Africa, Europe,

Provides EMC services for:
audio-visual equipment and educational/training aids; furniture; medical equipment; athletic footware; textile waste; pumps and valves.

Lotus Group, The

2411 Hamilton Mill Rd.
Charlotte, NC 28226

Phone: (704) 366-5505
Fax: (704) 366-0262

Contact: Abe Warshenbrot, President
Year Established: 1977

Foreign language capabilities: Spanish, French, Russian, Polish, Arabic, Hebrew
Geographic specialization: Worldwide

Provides EMC services for:
apparel, textiles, garment components and leather goods; chemicals, chemical and petrochemical industries equipment and products; construction equipment; furniture; graphic arts, printing equipment and supplies; hardware; optical, photographic, and scientific instruments; paints, varnishes and enamels; pharmaceuticals and hospital supplies; sporting goods; testing equipment. Also provides consulting services.

Piedmont Caribbean Trade Limited

3805 Bellevue Terrace
Gastonia, NC 28054

Phone: (704) 824-0452
Fax: (704) 824-0452
Cables: PIED CARIB

Contact: John J. Evans, President
Year Established: 1987

Foreign language capabilities: Spanish, French
Geographic specialization: Caribbean, South America, Africa, Europe, Far East, Middle East

Provides EMC services for:
apparel, textiles, garment components and leather goods; building materials; sporting goods.

International Marketing Systems, Ltd.

P. O. Box 806
Fargo, ND 58107

Phone: (701) 237-4699
Fax: (701) 237-4701

Contact: Allen W. Golberg, President

Year Established: 1979
Geographic specialization: Europe, Middle East, Africa, South America, Asia

Provides EMC services for:
farm equipment and products.

IVEX International
390 Main Street
Nashua, NH 03060

Phone: (603) 882-5460
Fax: (603) 881-8493

Contact: James K. McCormick, Executive VP
Year Established: 1987

Foreign language capabilities: Japanese
Geographic specialization: Japan

Provides EMC services for:
communication equipment and systems;
computers, peripherals, business equipment and
software; electrical, radio and TV, equipment and
parts.

Strong Trading Company
P. O. Box 151
Westmoreland, NH 03467

Phone: (603) 399-4994
Fax: (603) 399-7083

Contact: Donald A. Strong, President
Year Established: 1976

Foreign language capabilities: Spanish
Geographic specialization: Worldwide

Provides EMC services for:
games, toys, etc.; medical equipment; sporting
goods.

Symbicon Associates, Inc.
P. O. Box 896
Amherst, NH 03031

Phone: (603) 673-8898
Fax: (603) 673-1372

Contact: J. Buzzell, President
Year Established: 1980

Foreign language capabilities: German, French
Geographic specialization: Worldwide

Provides EMC services for:
communication equipment and systems;
computers, peripherals, business equipment and
software; industrial products and equipment;
medical equipment.

Agritech Products Int'l, Inc.
104 Harbor Drive
Jersey City, NJ 07305

Phone: (201) 433-6005
Fax: (201) 433-0241

Contact: Henry Abramowitz, President
Year established: 1975

Geographic specialization: Worldwide

Provides EMC services for:
food products and beverages; consumer products.

AME Matex Corp.
50 A & S Drive
Paramus, NJ 07653-0924

Phone: (201) 265-6500
Fax: (201) 265-6501
Telex 6853476 AME

Contact: Walter Prochorenko, President
Year Established: 1984

Foreign language capabilities: French, Spanish, Japanese
Geographic specialization: Pacific Rim, Europe, Far East, Middle East

Provides EMC services for:
air and water purification, pollution control and environmental control products and equipment; building materials; food processing/packaging machinery and equipment; hardware; heating, air-conditioning and refrigeration; lighting; paints, varnishes and enamels; restaurant, hotel and catering equipment; sporting goods.

Asia Minor Export Import Co., Inc.
64 So. Jefferson Rd.
Whippany, NJ 07981

Phone: (201) 515-9145
Fax: (201) 515-9144
Telex 136364 CORK WIPY

Provides EMC services for:
automobiles, accessories or parts; trucks, accessories or parts.

Bauer, Alex & Co.
2429 Vauxhall Road
Union, NJ 07083

Phone: (201) 964-4042
Fax: (201) 688-6668
Telex 138506

Contact: Leslie O'Brien, Sales Director
Year Established: 1945

Foreign language capabilities: Spanish
Geographic specialization: Latin America, Far East, Middle East

Provides EMC services for:
air and water purification, pollution control and environmental control products and equipment; heating, air-conditioning and refrigeration; industrial products and equipment; machinery and supplies.

C. International
P. O. Box 182
Hightstown, NJ 08520

Phone: (609) 443-5566
Fax: (609) 443-5566

Contact: Antonio Concepcion, Manager
Year Established: 1973

Foreign language capabilities: Spanish
Geographic specialization: Worldwide

Provides EMC services for:
accessories, luggage and jewelry; apparel, textiles, garment components and leather goods; games, toys, etc.; graphic arts, printing equipment and supplies; hardware; household furnishings and appliances; lighting; medical equipment; paper, packaging and containers; pharmaceuticals and hospital supplies; sporting goods.

Chazen Industrial Corp.
280 Midland Ave.
Saddle Brook, NJ 07662

Phone: (201) 794-1330
Fax: (201) 794-1663
Telex 642447

Contact: Henry Kessler, President
Year Established: 1974

Foreign language capabilities: Spanish
Geographic specialization: Worldwide

Provides EMC services for:
aircraft, accessories or parts; automobiles, accessories or parts; chemicals, chemical and petrochemical industries equipment and products; trucks, accessories or parts.

Creative International, Inc.
702 Paramus Road
Paramus, NJ 07652

Phone: (201) 358-6079
Fax: (201) 358-6532

Contact: Roger A. Chmelko, President
Year Established: 1988

Foreign language capabilities: French, Italian, Arabic
Geographic specialization: Europe, Middle East, Taiwan

Provides EMC services for:
medical equipment; pharmaceuticals and hospital supplies.

Davidson International
2055 Princeton Avenue
Westfield, NJ 07090

Phone: (201) 232-5921
Fax: (201) 232-5869
Telex 150153

Contact: William E. Davidson, President
Year Established: 1959

Foreign language capabilities: Spanish
Geographic specialization: Worldwide

Provides EMC services for:
consumer service industries: specialized machinery and equipment; electrical, radio and TV, equipment and parts; furniture; games, toys, etc.; household furnishings and appliances; pharmaceuticals and hospital supplies; sporting goods; cosmetics; beauty salon and beauty aid products.

Dreyco, Inc.
263 Veterans Blvd.
Carlstadt, NJ 07072-2792

Phone: (201) 896-9000
Fax: (201) 896-1378
Telex 620342 DREYCO
Cables: JAY DREYCO

Contact: Jack Dreyfus, President
Year Established: 1950

Foreign language capabilities: Spanish, German, French
Geographic specialization: Worldwide

Provides EMC services for:
automobiles, accessories or parts; gasolines, lubricants, and equipment; graphic arts, printing equipment and supplies; hardware; industrial products and equipment; marine and related products; sporting goods; trucks, accessories or parts.

SEE ADVERTISEMENT, PAGE 62.

Ewig, Carl F. Inc.
910 Oak Tree Rd.
South Plainfield, NJ 07080

Phone: (201) 756-3944
Fax: (201) 756-2575
Telex 229714

Contact: Stewart W. Tenner, Vice President-Int'l
Year Established: 1950

Foreign language capabilities: German, Spanish
Geographic specialization: Worldwide

Provides EMC services for:
aircraft, accessories or parts; apparel, textiles, garment components and leather goods; computers, peripherals, business equipment and software; consumer service industries: specialized machinery and equipment; household furnishings and appliances; medical equipment; marine and related products; optical, photographic, and scientific instruments; paper, packaging and containers; restaurant, hotel and catering equipment; time recorders and systems; testing equipment.

Exmart International, Inc.
Mt. Lakes Business Park, 115 Rte. 46, E3738
Mountain Lakes, NJ 07046

Phone: (201) 402-8600
Fax: (201) 402-8444
Telex 219018 XMART UR
Cables: EXMART

Contact: John L. McGrath, President
Year Established: 1980

Foreign language capabilities: Spanish, French
Geographic specialization: Worldwide, except North America

Provides EMC services for:
automobiles, accessories or parts; chemicals, chemical and petrochemical industries equipment and products; food processing/packaging machinery and equipment; household furnishings and appliances; restaurant, hotel and catering equipment; testing equipment.

Expo International Co., Inc.
P. O. Box 3477
Wayne, NJ 07470

Phone: (201) 956-7037
Fax: (201) 956-2120
Telex 6859565

Contact: Leonard M. Kahn, President
Year Established: 1980

Geographic specialization: Europe, Israel, India, Japan, Australia, South America

Provides EMC services for:
communication equipment and systems; electrical, radio and TV, equipment and parts; microwave components.

Expomar International Inc.
P. O. Box 1023
East Brunswick, NJ 08816

Phone: (201) 249-2302
Fax: (201) 249-2327
Telex 650-3512306 MCI UW

Contact: John P. McShane, Vice President, Sales

Year Established: 1982
Geographic specialization: Worldwide

Provides EMC services for:
air and water purification, pollution control and environmental control products and equipment; building materials; chemicals, chemical and petrochemical industries equipment and products; construction equipment; food processing/packaging machinery and equipment; medical equipment; pharmaceuticals and hospital supplies; trucks, accessories or parts. Also provides export trading company services.

Gas International Corp., The
670 Point Road
Little Silver, NJ 07739

Phone: (908) 741-1952
Fax: (908) 747-0172
Telex 4971854 (GASINC)

Contact: Gaston A. Schmidt, President
Year Established: 1979

Foreign language capabilities: French, Spanish
Geographic specialization: Worldwide

Provides EMC services for:
air and water purification, pollution control and environmental control products and equipment; communication equipment and systems; food processing/packaging machinery and equipment; food products and beverages; heating, air-conditioning and refrigeration; medical equipment; pharmaceuticals and hospital supplies; sporting goods; steambath and sanitary equipment.

General Product Co., Inc.
1969 Morris Ave.
Union, NJ 07083

Phone: (201) 687-4771
Fax: (201) 755-9053

Contact: Edward Wilkins, President
Year Established: 1980

Geographic specialization: Worldwide

Provides EMC services for:
accessories, luggage and jewelry; computers, peripherals, business equipment and software; electrical, radio and TV, equipment and parts; games, toys, etc.; household furnishings and appliances; novelties, gifts.

Gregg Company, Ltd., The
P. O. Box 430
Hackensack, NJ 07602-0430

Phone: (201) 489-2440
Fax: (201) 592-0282
Telex 134320
Cables: GREGGCAR HACKENSACK NJ

Contact: Harold Ross, President
Year Established: 1903

Foreign language capabilities: Spanish, French
Geographic specialization: Worldwide

Provides EMC services for:
materials handling equipment; mining equipment, minerals and raw materials; railway freight cars.

Hockman Lewis Limited
200 Executive Drive
West Orange, NJ 07052

Phone: (201) 325-3838
Fax: (201) 325-7974
Telex 13-8693 RCA 219189
Cables: PUMPMAKER

Contact: William S. Hockman, President
Year Established: 1932

Foreign language capabilities: French, Spanish, Danish, German
Geographic specialization: Worldwide

Provides EMC services for:
air and water purification, pollution control and environmental control products and equipment; farm equipment and products; gasolines, lubricants, and equipment; industrial products and equipment

SEE ADVERTISEMENT, PAGE 63.

Hoffman International, Inc.
300 So. Randolphville Rd.
Piscataway, NJ 08855-0669

Phone: (201) 752-3600
Fax: (201) 968-8371

Contact: Joseph F. Watters, President
Year Established: 1977

Foreign language capabilities: Italian, German, Russian, French, Filippino
Geographic specialization: Worldwide

Provides EMC services for:
construction equipment.

J & M Sales Corporation
P. O. Box 19
North Brunswick, NJ 08902

Phone: (908) 545-4600
Fax: (908) 545-8832

Contact: Jerry Schneiderman, Sales Director
Year Established: 1970

Foreign language capabilities: Spanish
Geographic specialization: Worldwide

Provides EMC services for:
automobiles, accessories or parts; construction equipment; farm equipment and products; trucks, accessories or parts.

JDRAS Enterprises, Inc.
(Source-Impex Div.)
75 Union Ave.
Rutherford, NJ 07055

Phone: (201) 933-6935
Fax: (201) 939-2772
Telex 496-04566 JDRAS-UI *Cables:* JDRAS

Contact: David S. Malka, President
Year Established: 1981

Foreign language capabilities: Polish, Russian, Italian, Spanish
Geographic specialization: Eastern Europe, Malaysia, Indonesia

Provides EMC services for:
air and water purification, pollution control and environmental control products and equipment; audio-visual equipment and educational/training aids; building materials; lighting; medical equipment. Also provides consulting services.

Kato International, Inc.
650 Springfield Ave.
Summit, NJ 07901

Phone: (908) 276-4405
Fax: (908) 276-4522
Telex 210961 KATO

Contact: Janusz A. Wolejko, President
Year Established: 1988

Foreign language capabilities: Polish, Russian
Geographic specialization: Eastern Europe, Southeast Asia

Provides EMC services for:
apparel, textiles, garment components and leather goods; audio-visual equipment and educational/training aids; electrical, radio and TV, equipment and parts; marine and related products; mining equipment, minerals and raw materials; pharmaceuticals and hospital supplies.

Kewanee International, Inc.
2429 Vauxhall Road
Union, NJ 07083

Phone: (908) 964-4040
Fax: (908) 688-6668
Telex 6853086 KWNEE UW

Contact: G. Robert Leiz, President
Year Established: 1971

Foreign language capabilities: Spanish
Geographic specialization: Far East, Middle East,
Latin America, Caribbean

Provides EMC services for:
heating, air-conditioning and refrigeration; industrial
products and equipment.

M & P Export Management Corp.
2329 State Hwy. 34, Suite 204/205
Manasquan, NJ 08736

Phone: (908) 223-0160
Fax: (908) 223-6745

Contact: Michael Oliu, Export Manager
Year Established: 1917

Foreign language capabilities: Spanish, Italian
Geographic specialization: Worldwide

Provides EMC services for:
furniture; games, toys, etc.; hardware; safety and
security equipment.

M. S. Universal, Inc.
499 Ernston Road
Parlin, NJ 08859

Phone: (201) 525-2208
Fax: (201) 525-1347

Contact: Mahmoud S. Abdel Baki, President
Year Established: 1982

Foreign language capabilities: Arabic
Geographic specialization: Middle East

Provides EMC services for:
automobiles, accessories or parts; chemicals,
chemical and petrochemical industries equipment
and products; electrical, radio and TV, equipment
and parts; food products and beverages; heating,
air-conditioning and refrigeration; household
furnishings and appliances; time recorders and
systems; trucks, accessories or parts; sealants;
adhesives; lubricants.

Medical International, Inc.
2000 First Ave.
Spring Lake, NJ 07762

Phone: (201) 974-1550
Fax: (201) 974-1554
Telex 362445

Contact: Carol Myers, President
Year Established: 1987

Geographic specialization: Far & Middle East,
Latin & South America

Provides EMC services for:
medical equipment; pharmaceuticals and hospital
supplies. Also provides export trading company
services.

Mondo-Comm Int'l Ltd.

17 Main St.
Bloomingdale, NJ 07403

Phone: (201) 492-2674
Fax: (201) 492-2936

Contact: Joseph Esposito, President
Year Established: 1986

Foreign language capabilities: Italian, German, Arabic
Geographic specialization: Europe, Middle East

Provides EMC services for:
automobiles, accessories or parts; consumer service industries: specialized machinery and equipment; industrial products and equipment; pharmaceuticals and hospital supplies. Also functions as a forwarding agent.

Muni Trading Co., Inc.

259 Amherst Ave.
Colonia, NJ 07067

Phone: (201) 815-0462
Telex 4933946

Contact: Nilesh C. Mehta, Vice President
Year Established: 1988

Foreign language capabilities: Hindi
Geographic specialization: Europe, Asia

Provides EMC services for:
apparel, textiles, garment components and leather goods; chemicals, chemical and petrochemical industries equipment and products; pharmaceuticals and hospital supplies.

Pegasus International Corp.

Straube Center K-2, 114 W. Franklin Ave.
Pennington, NJ 08534

Phone: (609) 737-3538
Fax: (609) 737-6829
Telex 650-342-8133 MCI UW

Contact: Donna L. McCabe, Sales

Provides EMC services for:
air and water purification, pollution control and environmental control products and equipment; chemicals, chemical and petrochemical industries equipment and products; consumer service industries: specialized machinery and equipment; industrial products and equipment; machinery and supplies; medical equipment; materials handling equipment; paints, varnishes and enamels; pharmaceuticals and hospital supplies; metals, tubing, wire.

Pennvint

2429 Vauxhall Road
Union, NJ 07083

Phone: (908) 964-4040
Fax: (908) 688-6668
Telex 6853086 KWNEE UW

Contact: Gerald D. Leonard, Managing Director
Year Established: 1986

Foreign language capabilities: Spanish
Geographic specialization: Far & Middle East, Latin America, Caribbean

Provides EMC services for:
materials handling equipment.

Strato Enterprises

7 Woodruff Road
Edison, NJ 08820-2601

Phone: (908) 549-4677
Fax: (908) 906-8197

Contact: Robert Kerman, Managing Director
Year Established: 1989

Foreign language capabilities: Dutch, German,
Mandarin
Geographic specialization: Southeast Asia,
Europe, Scandinavia

Provides EMC services for:
air and water purification, pollution control and
environmental control products and equipment;
aircraft, accessories or parts; chemicals, chemical
and petrochemical industries equipment and
products; communication equipment and systems;
computers, peripherals, business equipment and
software; industrial products and equipment;
machinery and supplies; testing equipment.

Sylvan Ginsbury Ltd.

P. O. Box 419
Oradell, NJ 07649

Phone: (201) 261-3200
Fax: (201) 261-2729
Telex 4754026
Cables: SYLVANDER ORADELL

Contact: M. Bacharach, Vice President
Year Established: 1920

Foreign language capabilities: German, Spanish,
French, Portuguese
Geographic specialization: Europe, Asia,
South America, Indian subcontinent

Provides EMC services for:
air and water purification, pollution control and
environmental control products and equipment;
aircraft, accessories or parts; communication
equipment and systems; computers, peripherals,
business equipment and software; electrical, radio
and TV, equipment and parts; industrial products
and equipment; machinery and supplies; optical,
photographic, and scientific instruments; high
technology electronic components.

Tecnomaster Int'l Corp.

161 Main St.
Hackensack, NJ 07601

Phone: (201) 342-5770
Fax: (201) 342-6746
Telex 424733

Contact: James H. Sandler, President
Year Established: 1980

Foreign language capabilities: Spanish
Geographic specialization: Europe, Far & Middle
East, Latin America, Australia, Africa

Provides EMC services for:
chemicals, chemical and petrochemical industries
equipment and products; construction equipment;
food processing/packaging machinery and
equipment; heating, air-conditioning and
refrigeration; machinery and supplies; materials
handling equipment; mining equipment, minerals
and raw materials.

Teleport Corporation

11-B Empire Blvd.
South Hackensack, NJ 07606

Phone: (201) 641-3660
Fax: (201) 641-6577
Telex 272587 TELPRT UR
Cables: TELEPORT HACKENSACKNEWJERSEY

Contact: M. S. Freedman, President

Year Established: 1960
Geographic specialization: Worldwide

Provides EMC services for:
automobiles, accessories or parts; trucks,
accessories or parts.

United International Marketing Corp.
64 Academy Circle
Oakland, NJ 07436

Phone: (201) 337-2255
Fax: (201) 337-1949

Contact: Eric Calder, President
Year Established: 1978

Foreign language capabilities: Spanish, German
Geographic specialization: Far East

Viking Traders Inc.
5 Cold Hill Rd. South, Suite 18
Mendham, NJ 07945

Phone: (201) 543-3211
Fax: (201) 543-9614

Contact: Steve Swanbeck, President
Year Established: 1986

Winters, J.C. Company
P. O. Box 190
Metuchen, NJ 08840

Phone: (201) 494-9428
Fax: (201) 549-6535
Telex 510-1003198

Contact: John C. Winters, President
Year Established: 1979

Foreign language capabilities: Spanish
Geographic specialization: Worldwide

**New Mexico Int'l Trade &
Development Co. (ITDC)**
4007 Comanche N.E.
Albuquerque, NM 87110-1082

Phone: (505) 881-2682
Fax: (505) 881-2682

Contact: Jess Hernandez, Jr., President
Year Established: 1986

Foreign language capabilities: Spanish, French, German
Geographic specialization: Latin America, Europe, Southeast Asia

vides EMC services for:
coverings.

---

vides EMC services for:
nes, toys, etc.; medical equipment; sporting
ods; gifts and novelties.

---

vides EMC services for:
dical equipment; pharmaceuticals and hospital
plies.

---

vides EMC services for:
cessories, luggage and jewelry; aircraft,
cessories or parts; apparel, textiles, garment
mponents and leather goods; building materials;
mmunication equipment and systems;
mputers, peripherals, business equipment and
tware; construction equipment; food
cessing/packaging machinery and equipment;
niture; mining equipment, minerals and raw
terials; paper, packaging and containers; safety
d security equipment; non-toxic insecticides.

KNOWN BY THE COMPANIES WE KEEP

Hockman-Lewis Limited has an unparalleled reputation for building international sales volume through existing and new distributors, which has provided the foundation for long term relationships with manufacturers we have represented exclusively for up to fifty-eight years.

From 1932 to the present, Hockman-Lewis Limited has concentrated on petroleum marketing, liquid handling, and automotive service equipment, sending its sales people to all areas of the globe from offices in the U.S.A., Europe, and Latin America.

We are always interested in strengthening our product groups with the addition of complementary equipment and to satisfy new requirements from our customers.

HOCKMAN-LEWIS LIMITED
200 Executive Drive
West Orange, New Jersey 07052 USA
Phone: 201-325-3838
Fax: 201-325-7974
Telex: 138693

313 R/E Ltd.
43 Argow Place
Nanuet, NY 10954

Phone: (914) 623-1630, (800) 833-1373
Fax: (914) 623-7180

Contact: Marion K. Rudaw, General Manager
Year Established: 1983

Foreign language capabilities: French, Spanish,
German, Italian, Dutch
Geographic specialization: Europe, Africa, South
& Central America, Pacific Basin

Provides EMC services for:
computers, peripherals, business equipment and
software; safety and security equipment.

A & S International Marketing Co., Inc.
77 Arkay Drive
Hauppauge, NY 11788

Phone: (516) 435-2999
Fax: (516) 435-2768
Telex 275793 ASIMUR

Contact: Abraham C. Abraham, General Manager
Year Established: 1980

Geographic specialization: Worldwide

Provides EMC services for:
air and water purification, pollution control and
environmental control products and equipment;
aircraft, accessories or parts; audio-visual
equipment and educational/training aids;
communication equipment and systems; farm
equipment and products; food processing/
packaging machinery and equipment; gasolines,
lubricants, and equipment; industrial products and
equipment; lighting; optical, photographic, and
scientific instruments; restaurant, hotel and
catering equipment; safety and security equipment;
testing equipment.

Acarex, Inc.
91-31 Queens Blvd.
Elmhurst, NY 11373

Phone: (718) 424-5551
Fax: (718) 424-8668
Telex 229311

Contact: Joseph Acar, President
Year Established: 1986

Foreign language capabilities: Spanish, French,
Turkish, Greek
Geographic specialization: Worldwide

Provides EMC services for:
automobiles, accessories or parts; chemicals,
chemical and petrochemical industries equipment
and products; construction equipment.

Actrade International Corp.
7 Penn Plaza, Suite 422
New York, NY 10001

Phone: (212) 563-1036
Fax: (212) 563-3271
Telex 6973434 ACI

Contact: Henry N. Seror, President
Year Established: 1988

Foreign language capabilities: French, Spanish,
German
Geographic specialization: Worldwide

Provides EMC services for:
air and water purification, pollution control and
environmental control products and equipment;
aircraft, accessories or parts; communication
equipment and systems; computers, peripherals,
business equipment and software; construction
equipment; farm equipment and products; games,
toys, etc.; gasolines, lubricants, and equipment;
hardware; heating, A/C and refrigeration; industrial
products and equipment; machinery and supplies;
paper, packaging and containers; restaurant, hotel
and catering equipment; dry-cleaning and pressing
machines; tufted carpets and rugs; lawn/garden
equipment.

New York State Announces
GEMS
Global Export Market Service

The Global Export Market Service (GEMS), a major component of New York State's Global New York Program initiated earlier this year, will provide technical financial and marketing assistance to small and medium-sized businesses or groups of businesses to help increase their sales by pursuing foreign market opportunities.

Assistance is in the form of matching grants to qualified firms (1) Export Diagnostic Assessments—an evaluation of organizational and/or product readiness for exporting; and, (2) Export Market Development Plans—will provide design and implementation strategies for firms or industry groups committed to beginning or increasing their export sales. Export Diagnostic Assessment and Market Development Plans will be conducted by private sector consultants selected on a competitive basis by participating firms in the GEMS program.

If you are a New York State firm or international consultant interested in participating in this unique program, call or write for full details to:

Global Export Market Services
New York State Department of Economic Development
International Division
1515 Broadway
New York, NY 10036 USA
(212) 827-6224

Ad. Auriema Inc.
747 Middle Neck Rd.
Great Neck, NY 11024

Phone: (516) 487-0700
Fax: (516) 487-0719
Telex 62402

Contact: Thom Masino, Advertising Manager
Year Established: 1921

Foreign language capabilities: French, Italian, Spanish
Geographic specialization: Worldwide

Provides EMC services for:
air and water purification, pollution control and environmental control products and equipment; food processing/packaging machinery and equipment; heating, air-conditioning and refrigeration; industrial products and equipment; medical equipment; mining equipment, minerals and raw materials; restaurant, hotel and catering equipment; electronic components.

AGB International Management Corp.
P. O. Box 238
Syracuse, NY 13214

Phone: (315) 445-2250
Fax: (315) 445-8909
Telex 937223

Contact: James A. Collins, VP - Marketing
Year Established: 1976

Foreign language capabilities: Arabic, French
Geographic specialization: Worldwide

Provides EMC services for:
building materials; construction equipment; heating, air-conditioning and refrigeration; industrial products and equipment; machinery and supplies; mining equipment, minerals and raw materials.

American Industrial Export Ltd.
44 Forest Rd.
Valley Stream, NY 11581

Phone: (516) 791-1991
Fax: (516) 791-5908
Telex 316233

Contact: Litza Schlanger, President
Year Established: 1981

Foreign language capabilities: German, French, Spanish
Geographic specialization: Worldwide

Provides EMC services for:
air and water purification, pollution control and environmental control products and equipment; marine and related products; safety and security equipment. Also functions as a buying service.

Amsco-Valley Forge
101 Corporate Drive
Hauppauge, NY 11788

Phone: (516) 435-1400/(800) 645-5604
Fax: (516) 435-1475
Telex 6852197
Cables: AMSCO

Contact: Salvatore J. Saccullo, Vice President

Provides EMC services for:
automobiles, accessories or parts.

Asch Trading Co.
415 Central Park West
New York, NY 10025

Phone: (212) 662-2186
Fax: (212) 222-8403
Telex 62579 ASCH

Contact: Bernardo Asch, President
Year Established: 1962

Foreign language capabilities: Spanish, French
Geographic specialization: South America

Provides EMC services for:
electrical, radio and TV, equipment and parts;
electronic parts.

Berns, M., Industries, Inc.
210 E. 86th St.
New York, NY 10028

Phone: (212) 744-4456
Fax: (212) 744-5276

Contact: Michael T. Berns, President
Year Established: 1976

Foreign language capabilities: Spanish, Italian,
Maltese, Farsi, German, Turkish
Geographic specialization: Worldwide

Provides EMC services for:
electrical, radio and TV, equipment and parts.

Bio-Livestock Int'l, Inc.
1 Blue Hill Plaza
Pearl River, NY 10965

Phone: (914) 620-0999
Fax: (914) 620-0005
Telex 510-1008754

Contact: Robert D. Langer, President
Year Established: 1985

Foreign language capabilities: Spanish
Geographic specialization: Worldwide

Provides EMC services for:
farm equipment and products; food products and
beverages; animal health products.

BMIL International
88 Pine Street (Wall Street Plaza)
New York, NY 10005

Phone: (212) 269-5700
Fax: (212) 269-4048
Telex 232072 KAYUR
Cables: FLEETINTL

Contact: Joseph Gervase, Executive Vice
President
Year Established: 1945

Foreign language capabilities: Spanish, Italian,
French
Geographic specialization: Worldwide

Provides EMC services for:
food processing/packaging machinery and
equipment; heating, air-conditioning and
refrigeration; restaurant, hotel and catering
equipment; cold storage equipment.

SEE ADVERTISEMENT, PAGE 76.

Browne International Industries, Inc.
401 E. 74th St., Suite 11N
New York, NY 10021

Phone: (212) 472-4725
Fax: (212) 472-4726

Contact: Jan P. Browne, President
Year Established: 1989

Geographic specialization: Worldwide

Provides EMC services for:
air and water purification, pollution control and environmental control products and equipment; construction equipment; industrial products and equipment; machinery and supplies.

Bryan, Errol H. International
P. O. Box 155
W. Islip, NY 11795

Phone: (516) 587-7979
Fax: (516) 669-1970

Contact: Mary H. Bryan Watts, President

Year Established: 1961
Geographic specialization: Worldwide

Provides EMC services for:
building materials; food processing/packaging machinery and equipment; restaurant, hotel and catering equipment.

Caravan Export Corp.
96 Atlantic Ave.
Lynbrook, NY 11563

Phone: (516) 599-9052
Fax: (516) 599-3743
Telex 233464THEO/UR

Contact: Theo Karavolas, President
Year Established: 1966

Foreign language capabilities: German, Turkish, Greek
Geographic specialization: Europe, Greece, Turkey, Middle East

Provides EMC services for:
automobiles, accessories or parts; chemicals, chemical and petrochemical industries equipment and products; communication equipment and systems; computers, peripherals, business equipment and software; construction equipment; consumer service industries: specialized machinery and equipment; farm equipment and products; heating, air-conditioning and refrigeration; industrial products and equipment; machinery and supplies; pharmaceuticals and hospital supplies; testing equipment; trucks, accessories or parts.

Celestial Mercantile Corp.
1600 Harrison Avenue
Mamaroneck, NY 10543

Phone: (914) 698-9187
Fax: (914) 698-1804
Telex 249566
Cables: "CELESTIAL"

Contact: Henry Simon, President
Year Established: 1950

Foreign language capabilities: German
Geographic specialization: Worldwide

Provides EMC services for:
accessories, luggage and jewelry; apparel, textiles, garment components and leather goods; automobiles, accessories or parts; games, toys, etc.; gasolines, lubricants, and equipment; hardware; paints, varnishes and enamels; pharmaceuticals and hospital supplies; sporting goods; trucks, accessories or parts; cosmetics; sewing thread; general merchandise.

Centrex, Inc.
38 West 32nd St.
New York, NY 10001

Phone: (212) 695-3320
Fax: (212) 967-1436
Telex 425221
Cables: CENTREX

Contact: Kenneth Cort, President
Year Established: 1938

Foreign language capabilities: Spanish, French
Geographic specialization: Worldwide

Provides EMC services for:
optical, photographic, and scientific instruments; sunglasses.

Charon-Jessam Trading Co. Inc.
117 Hudson Ave.
Freeport, NY 11520-6291

Phone: (516) 378-7354
Fax: (516) 378-7694
Telex 6852321 CHARON
Cables: CHARONFREE

Contact: Gene Colao, Director
Year Established: 1946

Foreign language capabilities: Spanish
Geographic specialization: Worldwide

Provides EMC services for:
automobiles, accessories or parts; construction equipment; marine and related products; trucks, accessories or parts.

Chew International (Div. Pan American Trade Development Corp.)
2 Park Ave.
New York, NY 10016

Phone: (212) 481-1800
Fax: (212) 696-5255
Telex 420429
Cables: ACTIVITY

Contact: Ralph Chew, President
Year Established: 1945

Foreign language capabilities: Spanish, Cantonese, French, Arabic, Mandarin, Tagalog
Geographic specialization: Worldwide

Provides EMC services for:
food processing/packaging machinery and equipment; food products and beverages; hardware; paper, packaging and containers.

Co-To Trading Corp.
15 Canal St.
New York, NY 10013

Phone: (212) 925-5926
Fax: (212) 226-1529
Telex 429537 COTOTRA
Cables: COTOTRAC NEW YORK

Contact: R. I. Cohen, President
Year Established: 1970

Foreign language capabilities: Japanese, some Chinese
Geographic specialization: Far East

Provides EMC services for:
medical equipment; optical, photographic, and scientific instruments; pharmaceuticals and hospital supplies; testing equipment.

Comtrade International Inc.

304 Kensett Rd.
Manhasset, NY 11030-2128

Phone: (516) 627-3033
Fax: (516) 365-8193
Telex 509 033 COMTRADE UD

Contact: Garbis I. Tabourian, President
Year Established: 1984

Foreign language capabilities: French, Arabic
Geographic specialization: Middle East

Provides EMC services for:
accessories, luggage and jewelry; apparel, textiles, garment components and leather goods; household furnishings and appliances.

Debco Chemicals Sales, Co.

140 East 2nd St., Suite 4L
Brooklyn, NY 11218
Phone: (718) 871-2484
Telex DEBKE MIO NY

Contact: Harold H. Rosenbaum, Director
Year Established: 1949

Geographic specialization: Worldwide

Provides EMC services for:
air and water purification, pollution control and environmental control products and equipment; aircraft, accessories or parts; chemicals, chemical and petrochemical industries equipment and products; farm equipment and products; graphic arts, printing equipment and supplies; industrial products and equipment; medical equipment; mining equipment, minerals and raw materials; optical, photographic, and scientific instruments; paints, varnishes and enamels; polarimeters and polariscopes.

Donovan, W. J. Co.

1200 Avenue of the Americas
New York, NY 10036
Phone: (212) 764-3496
Telex 667853

Contact: William J. Donovan, President
Year Established: *1947*

Geographic specialization: *Central America, Caribbean, Venezuela, Eastern Hemisphere*

Provides EMC services for:
air and water purification, pollution control and environmental control products and equipment; building materials; construction equipment; consumer service industries: specialized machinery and equipment; food processing/packaging machinery and equipment; safety and security equipment.

Dorian America
(Division of Dorian International Inc.)
2 Gannett Drive
White Plains, NY 10604

Phone: (914) 697-9800
Fax: (914) 697-9190
Telex 221856

Contact: Douglas Dunn, Vice President
Year Established: 1981

Foreign language capabilities: Spanish, French, German
Geographic specialization: Worldwide

Provides EMC services for:
food processing/packaging machinery and equipment; materials handling equipment; restaurant, hotel and catering equipment; commercial laundry and dry cleaning equipment.

SEE ADVERTISEMENT, PAGE 74.

Drake America

(Division of Dorian International Inc.)
2 Gannett Drive
White Plains, NY 10604

Phone: (914) 697-9800
Fax: (914) 697-9658
Telex 233310

Contact: E. S. Dorian, Jr., President
Year Established: 1947

Foreign language capabilities: Spanish, French,
German, Italian
Geographic specialization: Far & Middle East,
Latin America, Caribbean, Europe

Provides EMC services for:
automobiles, accessories or parts; building
materials; electrical, radio and TV, equipment and
parts; hardware; industrial products and equipment;
trucks, accessories or parts; lawn and garden
equipment and supplies; pumps and valves.

SEE ADVERTISEMENT, PAGE 74.

Dreyfus & Associates, Ltd.

509 Madison Ave., Suite 1400
New York, NY 10022

Phone: (212) 935-3250
Fax: (212) 758-7823

Contact: Steven Dreyfus, Director
Year Established: 1990

Foreign language capabilities: Spanish, French
Geographic specialization: Worldwide, except
Canada

Provides EMC services for:
automobiles, accessories or parts; hardware;
automotive service tools.

Duromotive Industries, Inc.

241 41st St.
Brooklyn, NY 11232

Phone: (718) 499-3838
Fax: (718) 788-8754
Telex 426706 DWEK

Contact: Roger Seti, Export Sales Director
Year Established: 1960

Foreign language capabilities: French, Spanish
Geographic specialization: Middle East, South
America

Provides EMC services for:
automobiles, accessories or parts; trucks,
accessories or parts.

Elmi Inc.

516 Fifth Ave., Suite 1003
New York, NY 10036

Phone: (212) 827-0130
Fax: (212) 575-5880
Telex 798270

Contact: M. H. Mahallati, President
Year Established: 1988

Foreign language capabilities: Farsi, Arabic
Geographic specialization: Worldwide

Provides EMC services for:
general merchandise.

EMB Trading Co.

P. O. Box 660
Schenectady, NY 12301

Phone: (518) 393-2233
Fax: (518) 393-2233

Contact: Morton V. Madison, Export Director
Year Established: 1950

Foreign language capabilities: French, German
Geographic specialization: Western Europe,
Scandinavia

Provides EMC services for:
aircraft, accessories or parts; communication
equipment and systems; electrical, radio and TV,
equipment and parts; industrial products and
equipment.

Empire Equities Inc.

109 Crane St.
Scotia, NY 12302

Phone: (518) 399-5362
Fax: (518) 399-2712

Contact: John T. Lang, President
Year Established: 1987

Geographic specialization: Eastern & Western
Europe, Pacific Rim

Provides EMC services for:
aircraft, accessories or parts; food products and
beverages; medical equipment; pharmaceuticals
and hospital supplies. Also provides financial
services.

Export Trade of America, Inc.

45 East 20th St.
New York, NY 10003

Phone: (212) 673-5000
Fax: (212) 777-6513
Telex 332934 EXPORT

Contact: Henry Lapidos, President
Year Established: 1981

Foreign language capabilities: Spanish, German,
French
Geographic specialization: Worldwide

Provides EMC services for:
apparel, textiles, garment components and leather
goods; food products and beverages; hardware;
household furnishings and appliances; paper,
packaging and containers; sporting goods.

Ferrex International, Inc.

17 Battery Place
New York, NY 10004

Phone: (212) 509-7030
Fax: (212) 344-4728
Telex 233-616 FREX UR

Contact: Sales Manager
Year Established: 1963

Foreign language capabilities: French, German,
Spanish, Italian, Portuguese, Russian, Mandarin
Geographic specialization: Worldwide

Provides EMC services for:
air and water purification, pollution control and
environmental control products and equipment;
building materials; farm equipment and products;
machinery and supplies; mining equipment,
minerals and raw materials; safety and security
equipment; welding equipment and supplies;
pipeline and industrial maintenance equipment.

SEE ADVERTISEMENT, PAGE 77.

Fischer Enterprises Inc.
1 North Lexington Ave.
White Plains, NY 10601

Phone: (914) 761-0022
Fax: (914) 761-0407
Telex 213716 FISH
Cables: FISCHENT NEW YORK

Contact: Harris E. Fischer, President
Year Established: 1988

Foreign language capabilities: Spanish, French
Geographic specialization: Worldwide

Provides EMC services for:
automobiles, accessories or parts.

Fleetwood International
88 Pine Street (Wall Street Plaza)
New York, NY 10005

Phone: (212) 269-5700
Fax: (212) 269-4048
Telex 232072 KAYUR
Cables: FLEETINTL

Contact: Joseph Gervase, Executive VP
Year Established: 1945

Foreign language capabilities: Spanish, French,
Italian
Geographic specialization: Worldwide

Provides EMC services for:
food processing/packaging machinery and
equipment; heating, air-conditioning and
refrigeration; restaurant, hotel and catering
equipment; cold storage equipment.

FMI Automotive Corp./
FMI Trading Corp.
100 Merrick Road
Rockville Centre, NY 11570

Phone: (516) 678-6444
Fax: (516) 678-6448
Telex 286610 FMI NY
Cables: AUTOPARTS/ROCKVILLE CENTRE

Contact: Miguel S. Fleischman, President

Foreign language capabilities: Spanish
Geographic specialization: Worldwide

Provides EMC services for:
automobiles, accessories or parts; chemicals,
chemical and petrochemical industries equipment
and products; industrial products and equipment.

SEE ADVERTISEMENT, PAGE 75.

Gate Group U.S.A., Inc.
75 Varick Street
New York, NY 10013

Phone: (212) 966-8995
Fax: (212) 966-8996
Telex 6971602

Contact: Ike Savitt
Year Established: 1980

Foreign language capabilities: Spanish, Russian,
Hebrew, Polish
Geographic specialization: Worldwide

Provides EMC services for:
graphic arts, printing equipment and supplies.

Geonex International Corp.

200 Park Ave. South, Suite 514
New York, NY 10003

Phone: (212) 473-4555
Fax: (212) 473-5925
Telex 960522 GEONIKINC NYC

Contact: Cynthia Tindale
Year Established: 1987

Foreign language capabilities: Spanish
Geographic specialization: Latin America, Far East, Middle East

Gerber, J. & Co., Inc.

855 Avenue of the Americas
New York, NY 10001

Phone: (212) 613-1100
Fax: (212) 613-1182
Telex 6716243

Contact: George Nikiforov, President
Year Established: 1937

Foreign language capabilities: French, Turkish, German, Spanish
Geographic specialization: Worldwide

Gilman Industrial Exports, Inc.

P. O. Box 93217
Rochester, NY 14692

Phone: (716) 334-5170
Fax: (716) 334-2395
Telex 978475 (GIEROC)

Contact: Philip F. Gilman, President
Year Established: 1975

Foreign language capabilities: Spanish
Geographic specialization: Latin America

Grand Pacific Finance Corp.

88 Pine Street
New York, NY 10005

Phone: (212) 425-0900
Fax: (212) 425-8252

Contact: Sherry Shen, Marketing Officer
Year Established: 1985

Foreign language capabilities: Chinese
Geographic specialization: Far East

Provides EMC services for:
air and water purification, pollution control and environmental control products and equipment; construction equipment; consumer service industries: specialized machinery and equipment; farm equipment and products; food processing/packaging machinery and equipment; gasolines, lubricants, and equipment; hardware; heating, air-conditioning and refrigeration; industrial products and equipment; restaurant, hotel and catering equipment.

Provides EMC services for:
air and water purification, pollution control and environmental control products and equipment; food products and beverages; household furnishings and appliances.

Provides EMC services for:
optical, photographic, and scientific instruments; industrial control instruments.

Provides EMC services for:
accessories, luggage and jewelry; building materials; chemicals, chemical and petrochemical industries equipment and products; communication equipment and systems; computers, peripherals, business equipment and software; hardware; industrial products and equipment; paper, packaging and containers; safety and security equipment; trucks, accessories or parts.

CORPORATION

FMI means Quality!

We represent worldwide selected leading manufacturers of:

☐ Automotive Replacement Parts and Accessories

☐ Service Station and Garage Tools and Equipment

☐ Industrial and Automotive Testing Equipment

☐ Spraying Implements and Chemicals

FMI means Service!

We put it all together:

☐ Multi-lingual sales executives travel the world over regularly

☐ Most competitive pricing

☐ Complete financing and credit terms

☐ Full consolidation of shipments to minimize shipping costs

☐ Personal contact with customers

For catalogs and information please contact:

FMI Automotive Corp.
FMI Trading Corp.

100 Merrick Road (P.O. BOX 401)
Rockville Centre, New York 11570

Cable: Autoparts/Rockville Centre
Phone: 516-678-6444
Telex: 286610 FMI NY
Fax: 516-678-6448

Hall & Reis, Inc.
94-39 44th Ave.
Elmhurst, NY 11373

Phone: (718) 458-2567
Fax: (718) 458-9249
Telex 424618 HARE UI
Cables: HALREIS NEWYORK

Contact: George Soukup, President
Year Established: 1951

Foreign language capabilities: German, Spanish, Italian, Portuguese, Czecheslovakian, Polish
Geographic specialization: Worldwide

Provides EMC services for:
building materials; chemicals, chemical and petrochemical industries equipment and products; construction equipment; consumer service industries: specialized machinery and equipment; farm equipment and products; hardware; heating, air-conditioning and refrigeration; industrial products and equipment; lighting; machinery and supplies; marine and related products; materials handling equipment; mining equipment, minerals and raw materials; safety and security equipment; sporting goods; oilfield and refinery supplies.

Hallmarkets International, Ltd.
26 Broadway, Suite 834
New York, NY 10004

Phone: (212) 668-0023
Fax: (212) 425-7776

Contact: L. Gavigan, Export Manager
Year Established: 1968

Foreign language capabilities: Spanish, Portuguese
Geographic specialization: Europe, Middle East, Latin America, Caribbean, Asia, Australia, New Zealand

Provides EMC services for:
computers, peripherals, business equipment and software; hardware; safety and security equipment; time recorders and systems.

Hardy, M. W. & Co, Inc.
111 Broadway
New York, NY 10006

Phone: (212) 964-1550
Fax: (212) 964-1553
Telex 235642 (HARDY UR)
Cables: HARDYACE

Contact: Philip Ashen, President
Year Established: 1947

Geographic specialization: Worldwide

Hyman, Harry & Son, Inc.
356 West End Ave.
New York, NY 10024

Phone: (212) 769-2860
Fax: (212) 799-5393
Telex 424191 (ITT)
Cables: HYMANEX-NEW YORK

Contact: Charles B. Hyman, President
Year Established: 1922

Foreign language capabilities: Spanish
Geographic specialization: Worldwide, except North America

IFRAS, Inc.

P. O. Box 4384
Great Neck, NY 11027

Phone: (516) 773-4093
Fax: (516) 466-8536
Telex 428562 IFRAS

Contact: Louis C. De Montarlot, President
Year Established: 1981

Foreign language capabilities: French, Spanish
Geographic specialization: Western Europe

Provides EMC services for:
accessories, luggage and jewelry; apparel, textiles, garment components and leather goods; automobiles, accessories or parts; building materials; food processing/packaging machinery and equipment; games, toys, etc.; medical equipment; marine and related products.

SEE ADVERTISEMENT, PAGE 80.

INSECO, Inc.

109 West 38th St.
New York, NY 10018

Phone: (212) 382-0702
Fax: (212) 391-7003
Telex 427084 INSECO

Contact: Mike Behmoaras, President
Year Established: 1984

Foreign language capabilities: Spanish, French
Geographic specialization: Worldwide

Provides EMC services for:
apparel, textiles, garment components and leather goods; automobiles, accessories or parts; chemicals, chemical and petrochemical industries equipment and products.

Provides EMC services for:
chemicals, chemical and petrochemical industries equipment and products; pharmaceuticals and hospital supplies.

Provides EMC services for:
hardware; household furnishings and appliances; giftware.

Inter Euro Trading, Inc.

432 Clinton St.
Brooklyn, NY 11231

Phone: (718) 834-9036
Fax: (718) 834-0390

Contact: Stephen V. Favorito, President
Year Established: 1990

Foreign language capabilities: Cantonese,
German, Hungarian, Italian, Spanish
Geographic specialization: Central & South
America, Eastern Europe, Far East

Provides EMC services for:
air and water purification, pollution control and
environmental control products and equipment;
apparel, textiles, garment components and leather
goods; building materials; electrical, radio and TV,
equipment and parts; furniture; medical equipment;
mining equipment, minerals and raw materials;
sporting goods. Liaison for legal consultation
regarding U.S. import/export regulations.

Intra-World Export Co., Inc.

286 Fifth Ave.
New York, NY 10001

Phone: (212) 736-4044
Fax: (212) 967-8517
Telex 232982 INTRA UR
Cables: DISTINCT, NEW YORK

Contact: Ram H. Balani, President
Year Established: 1953

Geographic specialization: Caribbean, Europe,
Western Africa, Middle & Far East

Provides EMC services for:
accessories, luggage and jewelry; apparel, textiles,
garment components and leather goods;
communication equipment and systems; games,
toys, etc.; hardware; household furnishings and
appliances; lighting; machinery and supplies;
optical, photographic, and scientific instruments;
paints, varnishes and enamels; paper, packaging
and containers; restaurant, hotel and catering
equipment; sporting goods.

Jahn, Henry R. & Son, Inc.

17 Battery Place
New York, NY 10004

Phone: (212) 509-7920
Fax: (212) 809-6422
Telex 222-070 EPI UR

Contact: Sales Manager
Year Established: 1914

Geographic specialization: Worldwide

Provides EMC services for:
air and water purification, pollution control and
environmental control products and equipment;
building materials; farm equipment and products;
machinery and supplies; materials handling
equipment; mining equipment, minerals and raw
materials.

SEE ADVERTISEMENT, PAGE 77.

Jitch, Harry & Sons

152 So. First St.
Brooklyn, NY 11211

Phone: (718) 384-3855
Fax: (718) 384-4646

Contact: John Dragonette, President
Year Established: 1982

Foreign language capabilities: Italian
Geographic specialization: Worldwide

Provides EMC services for:
food processing/packaging machinery and
equipment; games and toys.

Kalglas International Inc.
1170 Broadway, Suite 301
New York, NY 10001

Phone: (212) 683-5881
Fax: (212) 683-5883
Telex 423660 EXKA UI
Cables: EXKALGLAS

Contact: Bernard Broide, General Manager
Year Established: 1963

Foreign language capabilities: Spanish, French
Geographic specialization: Worldwide

Provides EMC services for:
food processing/packaging machinery and
equipment; games, toys, etc.; hardware;
restaurant, hotel and catering equipment. Also
functions as a purchasing agent.

Karl, Peter A. Int'l Sales Corp.
P. O. Box 824
Utica, NY 13503

Phone: (315) 736-8383
Fax: (315) 736-7817
Telex 93-7365 PAKARL NEML
Cables: "PAKARL"

Contact: Robert N. Hartman, Export Manager
Year Established: 1920

Foreign language capabilities: Spanish, French,
German
Geographic specialization: Worldwide

Provides EMC services for:
automobiles, accessories or parts; gasolines,
lubricants, and equipment; hardware; industrial
products and equipment.

SEE ADVERTISEMENT, PAGE 81.

Klockner Ina Industrial Installations, Inc.
666 Old Country Rd.
Garden City, NY 11530

Phone: (516) 794-1673
Fax: (516) 794-7397
Telex 823028

Contact: Klaus Brosig, President
Year Established: 1975

Foreign language capabilities: German
Geographic specialization: Worldwide

Provides EMC services for:
food processing/packaging machinery and
equipment; machinery and supplies; materials
handling equipment; mining equipment, minerals
and raw materials; restaurant, hotel and catering
equipment.

Kraemer Mercantile Corp.
49 West 23 St.
New York, NY 10010

Phone: (212) 206-0404
Fax: (212) 807-8324

Contact: Richard E. Seldon, Operations Manager
Year Established: 1922

Foreign language capabilities: Spanish
Geographic specialization: Worldwide

Provides EMC services for:
games, toys, etc.; household furnishings and
appliances.

Lanla Sales

30 West 26th St.
New York, NY 10010

Phone: (212) 645-2526
Fax: (212) 645-2533

Contact: Greg Haralampouois, Director of
Marketing
Year Established: 1978

Foreign language capabilities: Greek
Geographic specialization: Caribbean, Middle &
Far East

Provides EMC services for:
food processing/packaging machinery and
equipment; paper, packaging and containers;
gift-wrap items; disposable products.

Liberty Automotive Inc.

51-11 34th Street
Long Island City, NY 11101

Phone: (718) 786-2902
Fax: (718) 786-2909
Telex 422068 LIBAUTO

Contact: Richard A. Mezadurian, VP - Operation
Year Established: 1981

Foreign language capabilities: Spanish, Turkish
Geographic specialization: Middle East, South
America, Europe

Provides EMC services for:
automobiles, accessories or parts; trucks,
accessories or parts.

SEE ADVERTISEMENT, PAGE 86.

Magna Automotive Industries

999 Central Ave.
Woodmere, NY 11598

Phone: (516) 295-0188
Fax: (516) 295-0625

Contact: Manuel Davidson, Director - Export
Operations
Year Established: 1966

Foreign language capabilities: Spanish

Manhattan Nassau Corp.

P. O. Box 9
Valley Stream, NY 11582

Phone: (516) 872-8820
Fax: (516) 872-9726
Telex 6852034

Contact: Fred Berdach, President
Year Established: 1944

Foreign language capabilities: Spanish, French,
German
Geographic specialization: Worldwide

Meridian Synapse Corp.

210 E. 86th St., Suite 600
New York, NY 10028-3003

Phone: (212) 206-1920
Fax: (212) 691-9436
Telex 403820

Contact: Michael R. Cole, President
Year Established: 1974

Provides EMC services for:
audio-visual equipment and educational/training aids; medical equipment; optical, photographic, and scientific instruments; pharmaceuticals and hospital supplies; consumer products; infants' products.

Minthorne Int'l Company

747 Middle Neck Rd.
Great Neck, NY 11024

Phone: (516) 487-0700
Fax: (516) 487-3640
Telex 6852395

Contact: Paul R. Churchin, General Sales Manager
Year Established: 1921

Geographic specialization: Worldwide

Provides EMC services for:
chemicals, chemical and petrochemical industries equipment and products; communication equipment and systems; electrical, radio and TV, equipment and parts; medical equipment; marine and related products; optical, photographic, and scientific instruments.

Provides EMC services for:
automobiles, accessories or parts; trucks, accessories or parts.

Provides EMC services for:
electrical, radio and TV, equipment and parts; heating, air-conditioning and refrigeration; household furnishings and appliances; lighting; restaurant, hotel and catering equipment.

Morris Bros. Auto Trucks & Parts Corp.

150 Finn Court
Farmingdale, NY 11735

Phone: (516) 694-9161
Fax: (516) 694-9179
Telex 143146
Cables: MORBROPART, POWERAUTO NEW YORK

Contact: Ivan S. Simitch, President
Year Established: 1935

Geographic specialization: Worldwide

Provides EMC services for:
automobiles, accessories or parts; trucks, accessories or parts.

Moss, Paul E. & Company Inc.

515 Rockaway Ave.
Valley Stream, NY 11581

Phone: (516) 561-2555
Fax: (516) 561-2558
Cables: PAEMOSS

Contact: Louis J. Agnesini, President
Year Established: 1943

Foreign language capabilities: Spanish, French, Italian, German
Geographic specialization: Worldwide

Provides EMC services for:
automobiles, accessories or parts; chemicals, chemical and petrochemical industries equipment and products; gasolines, lubricants, and equipment; machinery and supplies; garage equipment.

SEE ADVERTISEMENT, PAGE 87.

Motorex Sales Corp.

2006 Grand Ave.
Baldwin, NY 11510
Phone: (516) 379-3310
Telex 221610
Cables: XEROTOM

Contact: H. Rodrigues, President

Provides EMC services for:
automobiles, accessories or parts; electrical, radio and TV, equipment and parts; trucks, accessories or parts.

New World Management, Inc.

1314 Gravesend Neck Rd.
Brooklyn, NY 11229

Phone: (718) 646-5900
Fax: (718) 646-5981
Telex 408649 NWM NY

Contact: Nicky Dozortsev, CEO
Year Established: 1987

Foreign language capabilities: Russian, Polish
Geographic specialization: USSR, Eastern Europe, Greece, Israel

Provides EMC services for:
apparel, textiles, garment components and leather goods; building materials; chemicals, chemical and petrochemical industries equipment and products; computers, peripherals, business equipment and software; industrial products and equipment; medical equipment; marine and related products; mining equipment, minerals and raw materials.

Nikiforov, George, Inc.

200 Park Ave. South, Suite 514
New York, NY 10003

Phone: (212) 473-4555
Fax: (212) 473-5925
Telex 960522 GEONIKINC

Contact: K. Robinson, Export Manager
Year Established: 1982

Foreign language capabilities: Spanish, French
Geographic specialization: Latin America,
Middle & Far East

Provides EMC services for:
air and water purification, pollution control and
environmental control products and equipment;
building materials; chemicals, chemical and
petrochemical industries equipment and products;
consumer service industries: specialized
machinery and equipment; food
processing/packaging machinery and equipment;
gasolines, lubricants, and equipment; hardware;
heating, air-conditioning and refrigeration; industrial
products and equipment; machinery and supplies;
restaurant, hotel and catering equipment.

On Time Development, Inc.

56-70 58th St.
Maspeth, NY 11378

Phone: (718) 417-5177
Fax: (718) 417-5192

Contact: Fred Sonneberg, Sales Manager

Provides EMC services for:
automobiles, accessories or parts.

Onyx Enterprises, Inc.

35-15 190th St.
Bayside, NY 11358

Phone: (718) 461-8608
Fax: (718) 939-8883
Telex 422813 TNIONYX
Cables: ONYXFENTER NEWYORK

Contact: Luis Martinez, President
Year Established: 1978

Foreign language capabilities: Spanish, Greek
Geographic specialization: Worldwide

Provides EMC services for:
audio-visual equipment and educational/training
aids; automobiles, accessories or parts; building
materials; chemicals, chemical and petrochemical
industries equipment and products; electrical, radio
and TV, equipment and parts; farm equipment and
products; food processing/packaging machinery
and equipment; heating, air-conditioning and
refrigeration; household furnishings and
appliances; medical equipment; pharmaceuticals
and hospital supplies; safety and security
equipment; scrap steel.

Prior, John Inc.

1600 Stewart Ave.
Westbury, NY 11590

Phone: (516) 683-1020
Fax: (516) 683-1024
Telex 421956 JONP UI

Contact: Ronald G. Prior, Vice President
Year Established: 1933

Foreign language capabilities: Spanish, French,
German
Geographic specialization: Worldwide

Provides EMC services for:
automobiles, accessories or parts; electrical, radio
and TV, equipment and parts; gasolines, lubricants,
and equipment; household furnishings and
appliances; paints, varnishes and enamels;
restaurant, hotel and catering equipment; trucks,
accessories or parts; lawn and garden equipment;
tools.

SEE ADVERTISEMENT, PAGE 88.

Proxima Inc.

P. O. Box 1071
New York, NY 10011

Phone: (212) 627-8572
Fax: (212) 627-8572

Contact: Carlos Vassallo, Director
Year Established: 1988

Foreign language capabilities: French, Italian,
German, Spanish
Geographic specialization: Worldwide

Provides EMC services for:
accessories, luggage and jewelry; apparel, textiles,
garment components and leather goods;
communication equipment and systems;
computers, peripherals, business equipment and
software; food products and beverages; graphic
arts, printing equipment and supplies; hardware.

Roburn Agencies Inc.

6 Executive Blvd.
Yonkers, NY 10701

Phone: (914) 968-1016
Fax: (914) 968-2188
Telex 238029 ROBR UR
Cables: ROBURNAGE

Contact: Peter N. Berns, President
Year Established: 1935

Foreign language capabilities: Spanish, French
Geographic specialization: Worldwide

Provides EMC services for:
communication equipment and systems; electrical,
radio and TV, equipment and parts.

Rodriguez, R.A., Inc.

320 Endo Blvd.
Garden City, NY 11530

Phone: (516) 832-2600
Fax: (516) 832-8083
Telex 221 711
Cables: RODICO, GARDEN CITY NY

Contact: Peter Rodriguez, VP - Marketing
Year Established: 1929

Foreign language capabilities: Spanish, French,
German, Italian
Geographic specialization: Worldwide

Provides EMC services for:
aircraft, accessories or parts; chemicals, chemical
and petrochemical industries equipment and
products; industrial products and equipment;
machinery and supplies; medical equipment;
optical, photographic, and scientific instruments;
testing equipment; trucks, accessories or parts.

SEE ADVERTISEMENT, PAGE 91.

Sharoubim International Group, Inc.

192-08 90th Ave.
Hollis, NY 11423

Phone: (718) 479-3011
Fax: (718) 479-3072
Telex 42376

Contact: K. Sharoubim, President
Year Established: 1968

Foreign language capabilities: French, Arabic
Geographic specialization: Worldwide

Provides EMC services for:
air and water purification, pollution control and
environmental control products and equipment;
aircraft, accessories or parts; building materials;
chemicals, chemical and petrochemical industries
equipment and products; communication equipment
and systems; computers, peripherals, business
equipment and software; construction equipment;
medical equipment; marine and related products;
materials handling equipment; pharmaceuticals and
hospital supplies; testing equipment. Also provides
consulting services.

National Association of Export Companies

If you're in exporting, you should be in NEXCO— the National Association of Export Companies. Our NEXCO membership benefits speak for themselves:

1. EDUCATION

Stay informed with the NEXCO Bulletin, our newsletter featuring industry news, notifications, tips, opinion and business leads.

Learn from targeted and timely presentations on exporter topics of interest at NEXCO luncheon meetings.

Gain from past NEXCO presentations at your own convenience through our audio and video tape collection.

Compare your results with the experiences of your peers through the new NEXCO survey of the exporting industry.

2. AFFILIATION

Network and interact for business, pleasure, and personal advancement in exporting.

Share common interests, experiences and opportunities among like-minded business people active in our industry.

Associate with the members of sister trade associations in the U.S. and in your foreign markets.

3. REPRESENTATION

Let us represent your exporter interests through our umbrella group, the National Federation of Export Associations (NAFEA) in Washington, DC.

Keep abreast of Washington legislative and administrative developments of importance to exporters.

Let us advocate your views and concerns at the Department of Commerce's Office of Export Trading Company Affairs (OETCA).

Call on our action for exporters with state and local government export promotion agencies.

4. CONNECTION

Benefit from our clearinghouse of contacts with EMCs/ETCs, export service vendors, and producers of exportable products

Join in our informal matchmakers to expand your network of export business contacts.

Gain more effective entree to export promotion programs at every level of national and state governments.

Use your NEXCO conduit to specialized and essential exporter services.

5. EXPANSION

Grow your business through our referrals to those contacting NEXCO about exporting events and assistance.

Develop international business opportunities through NEXCO multilevel contacts in the public and private sectors.

Increase your commercial impact through NEXCO's advocacy of trade intermediaries and export support vendors.

6. CERTIFICATION

Testify to your professionalism by displaying the NEXCO Certificate of Membership.

Add independent credibility to your letterhead and business cards with our authorized use of the NEXCO logo.

7. CONSIDERATION

Receive a FREE listing in Johnston's GUIDE to EXPORT and Johnston's DIRECTORY OF LEADING U.S. EXPORT MANAGEMENT COMPANIES.

Enjoy reduced subscription rates for export-industry trade magazines and publications.

Receive 5% off the cost of member ads in all Johnston International publications with the use of the NEXCO logo.

Get more **out** of exporting by getting **in**

National Association of Export Companies

**Call or fax Land Grant, NEXCO President—
Phone 516-487-0700 Fax 516-487-0719.**

Sheldon, H.D. & Company, Inc.

19 Union Square West
New York, NY 10003

Phone: (212) 924-6920
Fax: (212) 627-1759
Telex 420485   *Cables:* TENEKA

Contact: Nicholas C. Metros, President
Year Established: 1942

Foreign language capabilities: French, German, Spanish, Chinese, Portuguese
Geographic specialization: Worldwide, especially Europe and People's Republic of China

Provides EMC services for:
heating, air-conditioning and refrigeration; household furnishings and appliances; restaurant, hotel and catering equipment.

SEE ADVERTISEMENT, PAGE 89.

Silo International, Inc.

30 East 42nd St.
New York, NY 10017

Phone: (212) 682-4331
Fax: (212) 983-7074
Telex 224467

Contact: John P. Allen, Vice President, Sales
Year Established: 1969

Foreign language capabilities: Spanish, French, Italian, Portuguese, German, Hungarian
Geographic specialization: Worldwide

Provides EMC services for:
aircraft, accessories or parts; consumer service industries: specialized machinery and equipment; gasolines, lubricants, and equipment; hardware; heating, air-conditioning and refrigeration; household furnishings and appliances; industrial products and equipment; lighting; machinery and supplies; medical equipment; marine and related products; materials handling equipment; safety and security equipment; time recorders and systems.

Sterling International Corp.

41-26 27th St.
Long Island City, NY 11101

Phone: (718) 729-5550
Fax: (718) 729-5552
Telex 421421
Cables: INGSTERL

Contact: Henry A. Algava, President
Year Established: 1913

Tecnomasters International Corp.

254 West 54 St.
New York, NY 10019

Phone: (212) 581-9734
Fax: (212) 307-0272
Telex 424733

Contact: James H. Sandler, President
Year Established: 1980

Foreign language capabilities: Spanish
Geographic specialization: Worldwide

TRADECO Association of N.Y., Ltd.

260 Evergreen Ave.
Huntington Station, NY 11756

Phone: (516) 549-0851
Fax: (516) 757-5582

Contact: Terence W. Thompson, President
Year Established: 1985

Foreign language capabilities: French, Spanish
Geographic specialization: Europe

Provides EMC services for:
accessories, luggage and jewelry; air and water
purification, pollution control and environmental
control products and equipment; apparel, textiles,
garment components and leather goods; food
products and beverages; games, toys, etc.;
gasolines, lubricants, and equipment; lighting;
safety and security equipment; sporting goods.
Also provides consulting services.

Ultramar Agencies Co.

P. O. Box 402, Radio City Station
New York, NY 10101-0402

Phone: (212) 245-0315

Contact: L. M. Kruger, President
Year Established: 1946

Geographic specialization: Latin America,
Caribbean

Provides EMC services for:
Specializes in export trade development.

Provides EMC services for:
automobiles, accessories or parts.

Provides EMC services for:
air and water purification, pollution control and
environmental control products and equipment;
machinery and supplies; water pumps.

JOHN PRIOR, Inc.

International Marketing Management

In this globalized economy, the personal touch and service elements are more critical than ever for a manufacturer's success.

Based in the New York region for more than 50 years, JOHN PRIOR, INC. is one of the premier firms in the automotive aftermarket. Marketing personnel include 8 regional managers, 20 resident representatives and distributors in over 90 countries around the globe. The complete sales, marketing, merchandising and finance functions are handled on behalf of U.S. manufacturers.

In the past 8 years, the company has also formed separate sales divisions for restaurant and hotel equipment and lawn and garden equipment.

If you are interested in expanding your international horizons, please contact us:

JOHN PRIOR, INC.
1600 Stewart Avenue
Westbury, New York 11590 USA
Tel.: (516) 683-1020
Fax: (516) 683-1024

Universial Export Agencies
432 Park Ave. South
New York, NY 10016

Phone: (212) 532-1777
Fax: (212) 889-1894
Telex 425612 UNEX
Cables: VERSALEX Newyork

Contact: David E. Namias, President
Year Established: 1927

Foreign language capabilities: Spanish, German, French
Geographic specialization: Worldwide

U.S. Export Marketing Group
256 Oak Tree Road
Tappan, NY 10983

Phone: (914) 365-2800
Fax: (914) 365-2114
Telex 825951 USEX

Contact: John Freidman, Sales
Year Established: 1981

Geographic specialization: Europe, Middle & Far East

USExport, Inc.
52 Oliver Ave.
Albany, NY 12203

Phone: (518) 453-6015
Fax: (518) 489-8278

Contact: Louise Giuliano, President
Year Established: 1988

Foreign language capabilities: Japanese, Italian, Arabic
Geographic specialization: Japan, Middle & Far East

UTAC America Inc.
18 East 48th St.
New York NY 10017

Phone: (212) 223-0055
Fax: (212) 750-1146
Telex 662444

Contact: W. Nicholas Denton, General Manager
Year Established: 1963

Foreign language capabilities: French, Japanese, German
Geographic specialization: Europe, Middle & Far East, West Africa

Provides EMC services for:
accessories, luggage and jewelry; apparel, textiles, garment components and leather goods; games, toys, etc.; sporting goods; health and beauty aids.

Provides EMC services for:
medical equipment.

Provides EMC services for:
apparel, textiles, garment components and leather goods; heating, air-conditioning and refrigeration; industrial products and equipment; materials handling equipment; sporting goods; art and decorative items; new consumer products.

Provides EMC services for:
accessories, luggage and jewelry; air and water purification, pollution control and environmental control products and equipment; apparel, textiles, garment components and leather goods; automobiles, accessories or parts; building materials; food processing/packaging machinery and equipment; heating, air-conditioning and refrigeration; household furnishings and appliances; industrial products and equipment; lighting; medical equipment; optical, photographic, and scientific instruments; safety and security equipment; sporting goods.

Vanguard Int'l Management Services

245 5th Ave., Suite 2104
New York, NY 10016

Phone: (212) 725-2030
Fax: (212) 725-4554

Contact: Jeremy Davis, President

Year Established: 1987

Provides EMC services for:
computers, peripherals, business equipment and software; industrial products and equipment; machinery and supplies; paper, packaging and containers. Also provides consulting services.

Verde America, Inc.

93 Grand Street, #2
New York, NY 10013

Phone: (212) 431-6651
Fax: (212) 431-6693

Contact: Shunsuke Ueda, General Manager
Year Established: 1983

Foreign language capabilities: Japanese
Geographic specialization: Japan

Provides EMC services for:
air and water purification, pollution control and environmental control products and equipment; apparel, textiles, garment components and leather goods; building materials; construction equipment; furniture; industrial products and equipment; safety and security equipment.

Wedeen, Philip

240 East 27th St., Suite 21K
New York, NY 10016

Phone: (212) 686-0343
Fax: (212) 779-8670

Contact: Philip Wedeen, President
Year Established: 1985

Foreign language capabilities: Spanish
Geographic specialization: Latin America, Europe, Africa

Whittaker, Benjamin Inc.

1000 Park Blvd.
Massapequa Park, NY 11762

Phone: (516) 799-4716
Fax: (516) 799-4717
Telex 960864
Cables: BENWHIT

Contact: Matthew A. Schavel, President
Year Established: 1909

Geographic specialization: Worldwide

Wolfson, P. J. Co., Inc.

50 Kewanee Road
New Rochelle, NY 10804

Phone: (914) 235-3203
Fax: (914) 235-3203

Contact: R. Wolfson, Vice President
Year Established: 1945

Foreign language capabilities: French, German
Geographic specialization: Worldwide

Provides EMC services for:
aircraft, accessories or parts; audio-visual equipment and educational/training aids; building materials; computers, peripherals, business equipment and software; consumer service industries: specialized machinery and equipment; food processing/packaging machinery and equipment; graphic arts, printing equipment and supplies; heating, air-conditioning and refrigeration; industrial products and equipment; marine and related products; mining equipment, minerals and raw materials; restaurant, hotel and catering equipment; trucks, accessories or parts.

XPORT, Port Authority Trading Co.

One World Trade Center, Suite 35N
New York, NY 10048

Phone: (212) 466-3248
Fax: (212) 432-0297
Telex 427346 NYANDNJ

Contact: Herbert Ouida, Manager
Year Established: 1982

Foreign language capabilities: German, French, Italian, Spanish
Geographic specialization: Asia, Western Europe

Provides EMC services for:
air and water purification, pollution control and environmental control products and equipment; apparel, textiles, garment components and leather goods; building materials; chemicals, chemical and petrochemical industries equipment and products; communication equipment and systems; computers, peripherals, business equipment and software; food products and beverages; furniture; household furnishings and appliances; industrial products and equipment; lighting; medical equipment; pharmaceuticals and hospital supplies; forestry products.

Provides EMC services for:
carpet yarn; upholstery fabrics.

Provides EMC services for:
automobiles, accessories or parts.

Akron Overseas Inc.

P. O. Box 5418
Akron, OH 44333

Phone: (216) 864-6411
Fax: (216) 864-9300

Contact: Willem H. Adams, Export Manager
Year Established: 1964

Foreign language capabilities: French, German, Italian, Dutch
Geographic specialization: Western Europe, Japan

Provides EMC services for:
chemicals, chemical and petrochemical industries equipment and products; paints, varnishes and enamels; roof coatings.

Bock Pharmaceutical, Inc.

P. O. Box 785
Wilmington, OH 45177

Phone: (513) 382-5611
Fax: (513) 382-5611

Contact: James A. Bock, President
Year Established: 1964

Geographic specialization: North America, Middle East, Latin America, Caribbean, Asia, Australia

Provides EMC services for:
automobiles, accessories or parts; chemicals, chemical and petrochemical industries equipment and products; medical equipment; pharmaceuticals and hospital supplies; musical instruments.

Bogart International Sales

P. O. Box 42381
Cincinnati, OH 45242-0381

Phone: (513) 791-0595
Fax: (513) 791-0686
Telex 21-2072 RALBO UR

Contact: Raymond G. Bogart, Export Manager
Year Established: 1950

Foreign language capabilities: Spanish, French, German
Geographic specialization: Worldwide

Provides EMC services for:
apparel, textiles, garment components and leather goods; building materials; hardware; industrial products and equipment; safety and security equipment; sporting goods; trucks, accessories or parts.

Dunlap Export Co., Inc.

P. O. Box 5357
Akron, OH 44334-0357

Phone: (216) 864-2169
Fax: (216) 864-3544
Telex 4993577

Contact: Kathleen M. Washnock, International Sales Manager
Year Established: 1923

Foreign language capabilities: Spanish, French
Geographic specialization: Asia

Provides EMC services for:
automobiles, accessories or parts; chemicals, chemical and petrochemical industries equipment and products; household furnishings and appliances; medical equipment; pharmaceuticals and hospital supplies; trucks, accessories or parts.

SEE ADVERTISEMENT, PAGE 98.

Express Parts

17851 Englewood Dr.
Cleveland, OH 44130

Phone: (216) 234-8381
Fax: (216) 234-2660
Telex 810 4239438

Contact: Sales Manager

Provides EMC services for:
automobiles, accessories or parts.

Imtrex Corporation

3380 Tremont Rd.
Columbus, OH 43221

Phone: (614) 459-7790
Fax: (614) 459-7882
Telex 497-6561

Contact: Judith A. Vazquez, Export Manager
Year Established: 1987

Foreign language capabilities: Spanish, French,
Portuguese, Italian
Geographic specialization: Western Europe, Far
East, Latin America

Provides EMC services for:
communication equipment and systems; industrial
products and equipment; machinery and supplies;
mining equipment, minerals and raw materials;
pharmaceuticals and hospital supplies; foundry
supplies and equipment.

International Consolidated Exchange

P. O. Box 402
Dayton, OH 45449

Phone: (513) 294-4020
Fax: (513) 294-4020

Contact: Alan Doll
Year Established: 1987

Geographic specialization: Worldwide

Provides EMC services for:
audio-visual equipment and educational/training
aids; building materials; chemicals, chemical and
petrochemical industries equipment and products;
construction equipment; electrical, radio and TV,
equipment and parts; farm equipment and products;
heating, air-conditioning and refrigeration;
machinery and supplies; restaurant, hotel and
catering equipment. Handles all types of products.
Also provides consulting services.

International Projects, Inc.

5645 Angola Rd.
Toledo, OH 43615

Phone: (419) 865-6201
Fax: (419) 865-0954
Telex 650-372-6383
Cables: INTERPRO TOL

Contact: Michael Daum, Vice President - Export
Year Established: 1976

Foreign language capabilities: Spanish, French
Geographic specialization: Europe, Asia, Latin
America, Australia, New Zealand

Provides EMC services for:
food processing/packaging machinery and
equipment; furniture; heating, air-conditioning and
refrigeration; medical equipment; marine and
related products; restaurant, hotel and catering
equipment; sporting goods.

Intrade Inc.
3103 Executive Pkwy, Suite 402
Toledo OH 43606

Phone: (419) 534-3471
Fax: (419) 534-3477
Telex 284299 INTRADE

Contact: Kathi Burns, Manager
Year Established: 1982

Geographic specialization: MIddle East,
South America, Europe

Provides EMC services for:
automobiles, accessories or parts; disposable
medical products.

Marcus and Weimer, Inc.
190 East Washington St.
Chagrin Falls, OH 44022

Phone: (216) 247-3570
Fax: (216) 247-2132
Telex 6873052 MARUW
Cables: MARUS-CLEVELAND

Contact: Kevin L. Parker, Export Manager
Year Established: 1930

Geographic specialization: Worldwide

Provides EMC services for:
building materials; hardware; heating, air-
conditioning and refrigeration.

Natcom International
1944 Scudder Dr.
Akron, OH 44320

Phone: (216) 867-6774
Fax: (216) 864-7475
Telex 353739
Cables: "NATCOM-USA"

Contact: Frederick W. Nagel, Vice President
Year Established: 1978

Foreign language capabilities: German, French,
Spanish, Russian, Hungarian
Geographic specialization: Europe, USSR,
Hungary, Romania

Provides EMC services for:
air and water purification, pollution control and
environmental control products and equipment;
aircraft, accessories or parts; apparel, textiles,
garment components and leather goods; building
materials; communication equipment and systems;
computers, peripherals, business equipment and
software; food processing/packaging machinery
and equipment; games, toys, etc.; graphic arts,
printing equipment and supplies; heating, air-
conditioning and refrigeration; lighting; paints,
varnishes and enamels; paper, packaging and
containers; office supplies; plumbing supplies.
Also functions as an export trading company and a
consultant.

Ohio Overseas Corporation
520 Madison Ave.
Toledo, OH 43604

Phone: (419) 241-4334
Fax: (419) 241-5033
Telex 286041

Contact: Robert J. Devine, General Manager
Year Established: 1976

Geographic specialization: Middle East

Provides EMC services for:
audio-visual equipment and educational/training
aids; communication equipment and systems;
furniture; gasolines, lubricants, and equipment;
lighting; machinery and supplies; medical
equipment; optical, photographic, and scientific
instruments; paints, varnishes and enamels;
pharmaceuticals and hospital supplies; restaurant,
hotel and catering equipment; safety and security
equipment; time recorders and systems.

Pathon Company

4352 Brendan
North Olmsted, OH 44070

Phone: (216) 777-5333
Fax: (216) 777-6734

Contact: Paul J. Hruby, President
Year Established: 1976

Geographic specialization: Worldwide

Provides EMC services for:
industrial products and equipment.

Rivard International Corp.

10979 Reed Hartman·Hwy., Suite 200
Cincinnati, OH 45242

Phone: (513) 984-8821
Fax: (513) 984-8944
Telex 910 290 0089

Contact: Steven Mark Rivard, President
Year Established: 1988

Foreign language capabilities: French
Geographic specialization: Far East, Middle East

Provides EMC services for:
building materials; construction equipment;
hardware; industrial products and equipment;
paints, varnishes and enamels; trucks,
accessories or parts.

Taurus Shipping & Trading Co.

P. O. Box 24161
Cleveland, OH 44124

Phone: (216) 442-8764
Fax: (216) 461-0755

Contact: John Swanson, Director of Sales
Year Established: 1965

Foreign language capabilities: Spanish, French
Geographic specialization: Worldwide

Provides EMC services for:
automobiles, accessories or parts; industrial
products and equipment; trucks, accessories or
parts.

TradeCom International Inc.

33900 Curtis Blvd., Suite 208
East Lake, OH 44095

Phone: (216) 942-4468
Fax: (216) 942-2526
Telex 196183 TRADINT UT
Cables: TRADINT- CLEVELAND

Contact: Edward S. Benhoff, President
Year Established: 1970

Foreign language capabilities: Spanish, Italian
Geographic specialization: Worldwide

Provides EMC services for:
automobiles, accessories or parts; building
materials; chemicals, chemical and petrochemical
industries equipment and products; consumer
service industries: specialized machinery and
equipment; hardware; industrial products and
equipment; paints, varnishes and enamels;
pharmaceuticals and hospital supplies.

SEE ADVERTISEMENT, PAGE 99.

Tradex International
Div. of United Shippers
24600 Detroit Rd.
Westlake, OH 44145

Phone: (216) 899-1923
Fax: (216) 899-1925
Telex 275810 TRADEX UR

Contact: Saji Daniel, VP - Int'l Operations
Year Established: 1947

Foreign language capabilities: French, Spanish, Italian, Indian
Geographic specialization: Europe, Asia

Provides EMC services for:
building materials; chemicals, chemical and petrochemical industries equipment and products; computers, peripherals, business equipment and software; construction equipment; heating, air-conditioning and refrigeration; medical equipment; materials handling equipment; paper, packaging and containers; pharmaceuticals and hospital supplies; testing equipment.

Witz Scientific, Inc.
718 Illinois Ave.
Maumee, OH 43537

Phone: (419) 893-5368
Fax: (419) 893-8254
Telex 4997943

Contact: Kent Witzel, President
Year Established: 1983

Geographic specialization: Worldwide

Provides EMC services for:
air and water purification, pollution control and environmental control products and equipment; chemicals, chemical and petrochemical industries equipment and products; medical equipment; optical, photographic, and scientific instruments; pharmaceuticals and hospital supplies; safety and security equipment.

World-Trade Services, Inc.
2635 Noble Road
Cleveland Heights, OH 44121

Phone: (216) 382-8778
Fax: (216) 382-2743
Telex 980221 WORLDTRAD CLHS
Cables: WORLDTRADE

Contact: John H. C. Black, President
Year Established: 1960

Foreign language capabilities: German, French, Spanish, Arabic, Japanese, Chinese
Geographic specialization: Worldwide

Provides EMC services for:
apparel, textiles, garment components and leather goods; building materials; chemicals, chemical and petrochemical industries equipment and products; communication equipment and systems; construction equipment; electrical, radio and TV, equipment and parts; farm equipment and products; industrial products and equipment; machinery and supplies; medical equipment; pharmaceuticals and hospital supplies; safety and security equipment.

Zeller World Trade Corp.
P. O. Box 278
Defiance, OH 43512

Phone: (419) 784-3059
Fax: (419) 782-1939
Telex 286097 ALIEDESTIN DEFI

Contact: Randall C. Leiby, President

Provides EMC services for:
automobiles, accessories or parts; trucks, accessories or parts.

Products Corp. of North America, Inc.
310 S.W. 4th Ave., Suite 555
Portland, OR 97204

Phone: (503) 224-2424
Fax: (503) 241-8139
Telex 4949686

Contact: Fred Pfaffle, President
Year Established: 1965

Geographic specialization: Worldwide

Provides EMC services for:
building materials; farm equipment and products; food products and beverages; furniture; medical equipment; paper, packaging and containers; pharmaceuticals and hospital supplies; salvage items; inventory close-outs.

Third Party International
522 S.W. 5th, Suite 1400
Portland, OR 97204

Phone: (503) 248-9441
Fax: (503) 248-0126

Contact: Nicholai Vasilieff, President
Year Established: 1987

Foreign language capabilities: Hungarian, Russian
Geographic specialization: Worldwide

Provides EMC services for:
computers, peripherals, business equipment and software.

TWT International
P. O. Box 14276
Portland, OR 97214

Phone: (503) 231-7119
Fax: (503) 231-7512
Telex 360384
Cables: EXPORT

Contact: Robert L. Abraham, President
Year Established: 1980

Foreign language capabilities: Spanish, Portuguese, French, Chinese, Japanese
Geographic specialization: Worldwide

Provides EMC services for:
automobiles, accessories or parts; car washing and polishing equipment and supplies.

Allied Systems Export Corp.
12 W. Willow Grove Ave., Suite 181
Philadelphia, PA 19118

Phone: (215) 247-7740
Fax: (215) 248-9115
Telex 493-1621 (ISAPHA)

Contact: Isa Aharon, President
Year Established: 1970

Foreign language capabilities: Chinese, Japanese, Arabic, Hebrew, EEC languages
Geographic specialization: Europe, Middle East, Asia/Pacific, Africa, Australia

Provides EMC services for:
air and water purification, pollution control and environmental control products and equipment; chemicals, chemical and petrochemical industries equipment and products; consumer service industries: specialized machinery and equipment; food processing/packaging machinery and equipment; food products and beverages; industrial products and equipment; machinery and supplies; medical equipment; optical, photographic, and scientific instruments; pharmaceuticals and hospital supplies; safety and security equipment; testing equipment.

Ballagh & Thrall, Inc.

630 W. Germantown Pke., Suite 300
Plymouth Meeting, PA 19462

Phone: (215) 825-5710
Fax: (215) 834-1803
Telex 173145 BT UT

Contact: Jeffrey H. Susman, VP - Marketing
Year Established: 1933

Foreign language capabilities: French, Spanish, Mandarin, German, Tagalog, Italian, Polish, Farsi, Norwegian, Swedish, Danish
Geographic specialization: Worldwide

Provides EMC services for:
accessories, luggage and jewelry; apparel, textiles, garment components and leather goods; consumer service industries: specialized machinery and equipment; electrical, radio and TV, equipment and parts; food products and beverages; graphic arts, printing equipment and supplies; lighting; materials handling equipment; optical, photographic, and scientific instruments; paints, varnishes and enamels; safety and security equipment; time recorders and systems; testing equipment; wire; belting; acid-proof flooring; smoking goods; fluid handling equipment.

Davis Elliott International Inc.

801 Arch St.
Philadelphia, PA 19107

Phone: (215) 922-7475
Fax: (215) 922-7475
Telex 834778
Cables: BANDTEX

Contact: Charles H. Davis, President
Year Established: 1949

Foreign language capabilities: Spanish, German
Geographic specialization: Europe, South America, Asia, Middle East

Provides EMC services for:
air and water purification, pollution control and environmental control products and equipment; automobiles, accessories or parts; building materials; gasolines, lubricants, and equipment; graphic arts, printing equipment and supplies; industrial products and equipment; medical equipment; paints, varnishes and enamels; pharmaceuticals and hospital supplies; safety and security equipment; fire protection equipment.

Domestic & International Technology

115 West Ave.
Jenkintown, PA 19046

Phone: (215) 885-7670
Fax: (215) 884-1385
Telex 834635
Cables: DOMINTECH

Contact: Richard Stollman, President
Year Established: 1973

Foreign language capabilities: Spanish, German
Geographic specialization: South America, Southeast Asia, Middle & Far East, Africa

Export Consultant Service

108 S. Patton Dr.
Coraopolis, PA 15108

Phone: (412) 264-7877
Fax: (412) 264-4543
Telex 866705

Contact: Gerard F. Schweiger, Sr., President
Year Established: 1966

Foreign language capabilities: Spanish
Geographic specialization: Worldwide

Export Procedures Co.
309 S. High St.
Zelienople, PA 16063

Phone: (412) 452-6816
Fax: (412) 452-0486

Contact: Catherine E. Thornberry, President
Year Established: 1984

Geographic specialization: Worldwide

Provides EMC services for:
industrial products and equipment; machinery and supplies; hi-tech products.

Far East Trade & Investment Co.
351 Graham St.
Carlisle, PA 17013

Phone: (717) 243-0031
Fax: (717) 249-4468
Telex 510-600-7881

Contact: Tina Weyant
Year Established: 1986

Provides EMC services for:
industrial products and equipment; materials handling equipment; transportation equipment.

Provides EMC services for:
air and water purification, pollution control and environmental control products and equip.; automobiles, accessories or parts; building materials; chemicals, chemical and petrochemical industries equipment and products; construction equipment; consumer service industries: specialized machinery and equipment; food processing/packaging machinery and equipment; gasolines, lubricants, and equipment; heating, A/C and refrigeration; industrial products and equipment; materials handling equipment; mining equipment, minerals and raw materials; restaurant, hotel and catering equipment; safety and security equipment; testing equipment; trucks, accessories or parts.

Provides EMC services for:
air and water purification, pollution control and environmental control products and equipment; chemicals, chemical and petrochemical industries equipment and products; industrial products and equipment; optical, photographic, and scientific instruments; laboratory supplies and parts.

Fortune Enterprises International Co.

P. O. Box 1414
Hermitage, PA 16148

Phone: (412) 346-2722
Fax: (412) 346-1472
Telex 4998015 FEICO

Contact: Jong-Sen Hsu, President
Year Established: 1981

Foreign language capabilities: Chinese,
Taiwanese, Japanese
Geographic specialization: Southeast Asia, China,
Taiwan

Provides EMC services for:
electrical, radio and TV, equipment and parts;
industrial products and equipment; machinery and
supplies.

Handforth Company, The

678 S. Aubrey St.
Allentown, PA 18103

Phone: (215) 772-7660
Fax: (215) 433-2246
Telex 312897 HANDFORTH

Contact: Geoffrey H. Reis, President
Year Established: 1985

Foreign language capabilities: French
Geographic specialization: Europe (especially
Netherlands), Australia

Provides EMC services for:
automobiles, accessories or parts.

IBEX Technical Corp.

113 Orchard Hilands Dr.
Venetia, PA 15367

Phone: (412) 941-4808
Fax: (412) 941-4101
Telex 291919

Contact: Hugh Cameron, President
Year Established: 1979

Geographic specialization: Worldwide

Provides EMC services for:
automobiles, accessories or parts; electrical, radio
and TV, equipment and parts; industrial products
and equipment; medical equipment; optical,
photographic, and scientific instruments; time
recorders and systems; testing equipment.

International Controls Co., Inc.

P. O. Box 306
Warrington, PA 18976

Phone: (215) 343-2707
Fax: (215) 343-3009
Telex 4761227

Contact: Sager T. Colman, President
Year Established: 1964

Foreign language capabilities: Spanish,
Portuguese, German
Geographic specialization: Central & South
America, Caribbean, Pacific Rim, Europe

Provides EMC services for:
air and water purification, pollution control and
environmental control products and equipment;
chemicals, chemical and petrochemical industries
equipment and products; computers, peripherals,
business equipment and software; industrial
products and equipment; optical, photographic, and
scientific instruments; testing equipment.

Jireh International

P. O. Box 696
Chester, PA 19016

Phone: (215) 872-3396
Fax: (215) 627-5427
Telex 940103 WUPUBTLXBSN
Cables: JIREH, PA

Contact: William L. Scott, President
Year Established: 1989

Provides EMC services for:
farm equipment and products; medical equipment.

Matthews Globus Trading, Ltd.

1951 Brinton Rd.
York, PA 17405

Phone: (717) 764-2345

Contact: James Pickard, Vice President

Geographic specialization: Worldwide

Provides EMC services for:
graphic arts, printing equipment and supplies;
paper, packaging and containers.

Mercator Corporation

728 Penn Ave.
West Reading, PA 19611

Phone: (215) 376-1578
Fax: (215) 376-5053
Telex 836420 MERCATOR RDG
Cables: MERCATOR READING

Contact: Philip C. Klein, President
Year Established: 1946

Foreign language capabilities: Spanish
Geographic specialization: Western Hemisphere,
Western Europe, Middle East, Africa, Pakistan,
India, Pacific Rim

Provides EMC services for:
air and water purification, pollution control and
environmental control products and equipment;
farm equipment and products; food
processing/packaging machinery and equipment;
heating, air-conditioning and refrigeration; industrial
products and equipment; materials handling
equipment; compressed air dryers; valves;
turbines.

State Export Corporation

535 W. Germantown Pike
Norristown, PA 19403

Phone: (215) 277-8700
Fax: (215) 277-8700 Ext. 231
Telex 83-4467
Cables: STATEXPOR NTW

Contact: Federico A. Scheel, Vice President
Year Established: 1946

Geographic specialization: Worldwide

Provides EMC services for:
automobiles, accessories or parts; industrial
products and equipment.

Trans International Group Ltd.

18 Sentry Parkway-Suite 1
Blue Bell, PA 19422

Phone: (215) 549-2295
Fax: (215) 540-2290
Cables: "EXDEP"/Philadelphia, PA

Contact: Anthony M. Swartz, President
Year Established: 1976

Foreign language capabilities: Spanish, Portuguese
Geographic specialization: Caribbean, Latin America, Pacific Rim, Europe, Middle East

Provides EMC services for:
electrical, radio and TV, equipment and parts; food processing/packaging machinery and equipment; food products and beverages; general consumer products.

International Industries Corp.

P. O. Box 1193
Spartanburg, SC 29304

Phone: (803) 439-4040
Fax: (803) 439-6300

Contact: David W. Cloer, President
Year Established: 1976

Geographic specialization: Middle & Far East, Latin America, Europe, Caribbean

Provides EMC services for:
apparel, textiles, garment components and leather goods; automobiles, accessories or parts; chemicals, chemical and petrochemical industries equipment and products; food products and beverages.

Latco International, Inc.

P. O. Box 27
Orangeburg, SC 29116-0027

Phone: (803) 536-6973
Fax: (803) 536-6973
Telex 988502 LATCO SC UD

Contact: L. A. Talero, President
Year Established: 1976

Foreign language capabilities: Spanish, French, Portuguese, Italian

Provides EMC services for:
aircraft, accessories or parts; hardware; industrial products and equipment; machinery and supplies; materials handling equipment.

Embree, C. A. Co.

P. O. Box 111209
Nashville, TN 37211

Phone: (615) 832-0306

Contact: Chester A. Embree, President

Year Established: 1963

Geographic specialization: Europe, Far East

Provides EMC services for:
apparel, textiles, garment components and leather goods; sporting goods; sport and casual clothing. Provides broker/representative services.

Technic Group
1215 Clermont Dr.
Chattanooga, TN 37415

Phone: (615) 875-9840
Fax: (615) 877-0017

Contact: William J. Laudeman, President
Year Established: 1987

Geographic specialization: Worldwide

Provides EMC services for:
air and water purification, pollution control and environmental control products and equipment; aircraft, accessories or parts; audio-visual equipment and educational/training aids; chemicals, chemical and petrochemical industries equipment and products; communication equipment and systems; construction equipment; farm equipment and products; food processing/packaging machinery and equipment; industrial products and equipment; machinery and supplies; medical equipment; marine and related products; materials handling equipment.

Automotive International Corp.
World Trade Center, Box 58766
Dallas, TX 75258

Phone: (214) 634-2900
Fax: (214) 634-3364
Telex 730841
Cables: AICDAL

Contact: Marshall D. Gardner, President
Year Established: 1978

Foreign language capabilities: German, Spanish

Provides EMC services for:
aircraft, accessories or parts; automobiles, accessories or parts; computers, peripherals, business equipment and software; construction equipment; farm equipment and products; mining equipment, minerals and raw materials; trucks, accessories or parts.

Comanache Moon Trading Co.
1104 West Ave., Suite 103
Austin, TX 78701

Phone: (512) 478-6670
Fax: (512) 478-0920

Contact: R. J. Brimble, President
Year Established: 1989

Foreign language capabilities: French, German, Spanish
Geographic specialization: Europe, Australia, New Zealand

Provides EMC services for:
accessories, luggage and jewelry; apparel, textiles, garment components and leather goods.

Fame International
P. O. Box 5066
El Paso, TX 79953

Phone: (915) 772-4579
Fax: (915) 772-4649
Telex 74-9328
Cables: FAME

Contact: Ruben Perex, Export Manager
Year Established: 1974

Foreign language capabilities: Spanish, French, Italian, Portuguese
Geographic specialization: Latin America, Caribbean

Provides EMC services for:
air and water purification, pollution control and environmental control products and equipment; chemicals, chemical and petrochemical industries equipment and products; computers, peripherals, business equipment and software; food processing/packaging machinery and equipment.

First Gulf International, Inc.

11500 N.W. Freeway #410
Houston, TX 77092

Phone: (713) 688-0397
Fax: (713) 681-6502
Cables: FGICO

Contact: Martin Hamouie, Marketing Manager
Year Established: 1981

Foreign language capabilities: Arabic
Geographic specialization: Latin America, Middle East, North Africa

Provides EMC services for:
medical equipment; materials handling equipment; optical, photographic, and scientific instruments; pharmaceuticals and hospital supplies.

Globelink Incorporated

World Trade Center, Box 58022
Dallas, TX 75258

Phone: (214) 761-5670
Fax: (214) 761-5670

Contact: Milan Vesely, International Director
Year Established: 1970

Foreign language capabilities: Spanish, French, Swahili
Geographic specialization: Worldwide

Provides EMC services for:
accessories, luggage and jewelry; aircraft, accessories or parts; audio-visual equipment and educational/training aids; chemicals, chemical and petrochemical industries equipment and products; communication equipment and systems; consumer service industries: specialized machinery and equipment; furniture; games, toys, etc.; hardware; household furnishings and appliances; lighting; materials handling equipment; restaurant, hotel and catering equipment; commercial fishing equipment.

Import Export Management Service, Inc.

P. O. Box 59309
Dallas, TX 75229

Phone: (214) 620-9545
Fax: (214) 243-4627

Contact: Yvonne-Monique Engels, Vice President
Year Established: 1967

Foreign language capabilities: German, Spanish, French
Geographic specialization: Worldwide

Provides EMC services for:
audio-visual equipment and educational/training aids; chemicals, chemical and petrochemical industries equipment and products; computers, peripherals, business equipment and software; furniture; games, toys, etc.; graphic arts, printing equipment and supplies; paints, varnishes and enamels; paper, packaging and containers; office supplies; engineering and drafting supplies.

ITBR, Inc.

P. O. Box 160325
Austin, TX 78716

Phone: (512) 329-2170

Contact: Ernest Chavarria, President
Year Established: 1977

Foreign language capabilities: Spanish, Italian
Geographic specialization: Latin America, Canada, Europe

Provides EMC services for:
aircraft, accessories or parts; audio-visual equipment and educational/training aids; building materials; chemicals, chemical and petrochemical industries equipment and products; communication equipment and systems; electrical, radio and TV, equipment and parts; food processing/packaging machinery and equipment; medical equipment; mining equipment, minerals and raw materials; paper, packaging and containers; restaurant, hotel and catering equipment; safety and security equipment; trucks, accessories or parts.

Pacific Export Services, Inc.
3500 Maple Ave., Suite 1465
Dallas, TX 75219

Phone: (214) 521-5521
Fax: (214) 521-7010

Contact: Stanley E. Marcus, COO
Year Established: 1987

Foreign language capabilities: Japanese
Geographic specialization: Japan

Provides EMC services for:
accessories, luggage and jewelry; apparel, textiles,
garment components and leather goods; audio-
visual equipment and educational/training aids;
communication equipment and systems;
computers, peripherals, business equipment and
software; construction equipment; furniture;
games, toys, etc.; household furnishings and
appliances; marine and related products; sporting
goods; time recorders and systems. Handles all
types of products for export to Japan.

American Trade International Corp.
P. O. Box 17885
Salt Lake City, UT 84117

Phone: (801) 272-9145
Fax: (801) 350-9051
Telex 910 240 4492 TOS SLC

Contact: Robert A. Slater, President
Year Established: 1979

Foreign language capabilities: Spanish,
Portuguese, Japanese
Geographic specialization: Europe, Latin America,
Asia

Provides EMC services for:
automobiles, accessories or parts; food products
and beverages; furniture; household furnishings
and appliances; medical equipment.

Asia Marketing & Consulting Corp.
5243 Carpell Ave.
Salt Lake City, UT 84118-8044

Phone: (801) 964-2825
Fax: (801) 964-0551

Contact: George M. McCune, CEO
Year Established: 1983

Foreign language capabilities: Japanese,
Chinese, Korean, Thai, Indonesian, Malay
Geographic specialization: Orient, Pacific Rim

Provides EMC services for:
accessories, luggage and jewelry; aircraft,
accessories or parts; automobiles, accessories or
parts; chemicals, chemical and petrochemical
industries equipment and products; construction
equipment; electrical, radio and TV, equipment and
parts; food processing/packaging machinery and
equipment; furniture; machinery and supplies.
Also provides consulting services regarding
franchise opportunities, translation and
interpreting.

ISIS International Export Management Co.
P. O. Box 685
Salt Lake City, UT 84110-0685

Phone: (801) 583-4213
Fax: (801) 583-6606

Contact: Nohman El-Meligi, President
Year Established: 1989

Foreign language capabilities: Arabic, French
Geographic specialization: Arab world, Canada,
French-speaking countries

Provides EMC services for:
automobiles, accessories or parts; building
materials; computers, peripherals, business
equipment and software; consumer service
industries: specialized machinery and equipment;
food processing/packaging machinery and
equipment; food products and beverages;
household furnishings and appliances; machinery
and supplies; marine and related products; mining
equipment, minerals and raw materials; paper,
packaging and containers.

HCI Corporation

10 E. Washington St.
Lexington, VA 24450

Phone: (703) 463-1095
Fax: (703) 463-1095
Telex 685 1243 HCI

Contact: Hugh M. Henderson, President
Year Established: 1976

Foreign language capabilities: French, German, Chinese, Spanish
Geographic specialization: Latin America, Pacific Rim, Western Europe

Provides EMC services for:
air and water purification, pollution control and environmental control products and equipment; chemicals, chemical and petrochemical industries equipment and products; farm equipment and products; food products and beverages; medical equipment; biological technology.

M International Export (MINTEX)

3504 Redwood Cover
Fairfax, VA 22030

Phone: (703) 243-0200
Fax: (703) 525-5715
Telex 64112 MINTEX

Contact: Peter J. Nebb, Director of Marketing
Year Established: 1977

Foreign language capabilities: French, German, Arabic, Spanish, Thai, Italian
Geographic specialization: Europe, North America, Middle & Far East

Provides EMC services for:
air and water purification, pollution control and environmental control products and equipment; aircraft, accessories or parts; communication equipment and systems; aircraft engine/component overhaul.

Tradeways, Ltd.

307-F Maple Ave. West
Vienna, VA 22180

Phone: (703) 281-5482
Fax: (703) 281-5167
Telex 197924

Contact: Joseph G. Gorski, President

Geographic specialization: Europe, Middle & Far East

Provides EMC services for:
audio-visual equipment and educational/training aids; electrical, radio and TV, equipment and parts; food processing/packaging machinery and equipment; testing equipment.

Boar's Head Int'l Trading Co., Ltd. (Ind. Division)

P. O. Box 7146
Lynnwood, WA 98046

Phone: (206) 775-2332
Fax: (206) 775-2333
Telex 823012 BOARS UF

Contact: James P. Surdyke, Managing Director
Year Established: 1980

Foreign language capabilities: Chinese, Spanish
Geographic specialization: Pacific Rim, South & Central America

Provides EMC services for:
air and water purification, pollution control and environmental control products and equipment; chemicals, chemical and petrochemical industries equipment and products; computers, peripherals, business equipment and software; consumer service industries: specialized machinery and equipment; food processing/packaging machinery and equipment; lighting; medical equipment; restaurant, hotel and catering equipment; time recorders and systems.

International Marketing Services Co.

518 1st. Ave. N. #22
Seattle, WA 98109

Phone: (206) 284-0886
Fax: (206) 633-4730
Telex 213944 IMSCO UR

Contact: J. Murphy, Manager
Year Established: 1969

Geographic specialization: Pacific Rim

Provides EMC services for:
air and water purification, pollution control and
environmental control products and equipment;
communication equipment and systems;
computers, peripherals, business equipment and
software; electrical, radio and TV, equipment and
parts.

Internet Corporation USA

P. O. Box 98328
Tacoma, WA 98498

Phone: (206) 535-3803
Fax: (206) 531-5123
Telex 940103

Contact: Ronald W. Ehli, President
Year Established: 1988

Geographic specialization: Worldwide

Provides EMC services for:
building materials; food products and beverages;
furniture.

Jajin Trading and Marketing, Inc.

13240 Northup Way, Suite 18A
Bellevue, WA 98005

Phone: (206) 641-1064
Fax: (206) 641-6426

Contact: J. M. Koslosky, President
Year Established: 1989

Foreign language capabilities: French, Russian,
Slovak
Geographic specialization: Pacific Rim, Europe

Provides EMC services for:
air and water purification, pollution control and
environmental control products and equipment;
apparel, textiles, garment components and leather
goods; building materials; food products and
beverages; lighting; paper, packaging and
containers. Also provides consulting services.

Pac-Rim Im-Ex

10335 N.E. 141st St.
Bothell, WA 98011

Phone: (206) 821-9264

Contact: Barry S. Hogrefe, President

Year Established: 1989
Geographic specialization: Pacific Rim, Australia

Provides EMC services for:
automobiles, accessories or parts; building
materials; food products and beverages.

Saris Corp.

1258 First Ave. South, Suite 406
Seattle, WA 98134

Phone: (206) 340-1835
Fax: (206) 340-1836

Contact: Russell H. Bennett, President
Year Established: 1988

Foreign language capabilities: French, Spanish,
Korean, Japanese
Geographic specialization: South America, Pacific
Rim

Provides EMC services for:
building materials; farm equipment and products;
industrial products and equipment. Provides export
trading company services.

Borco Engineering Co.

5654 Pennwall St.
Madison, WI 53711

Phone: (608) 271-1887

Contact: Lee R. Haspl, General Manager
Year Established: 1969

Foreign language capabilities: Czecheslovakian,
Spanish
Geographic specialization: Europe, Middle & Far
East, Latin America, Africa

Provides EMC services for:
food processing/packaging machinery and
equipment; industrial products and equipment;
machinery and supplies; testing equipment.

McLean International Marketing, Inc.

P. O. Box 535
Mequon, WI 53092

Phone: (414) 242-0958
Fax: (414) 242-6644
Telex via MCI 6730453

Contact: Samuel E. Greeley, President
Year Established: 1979

Foreign language capabilities: Spanish
Geographic specialization: Southeast Asia,
Middle & Far East

Provides EMC services for:
apparel, textiles, garment components and leather
goods; construction equipment; farm equipment
and products; food processing/packaging
machinery and equipment; furniture; industrial
products and equipment; machinery and supplies;
safety and security equipment.

Midwest Agricultural Export Corp.

P. O. Box 865
Madison, WI 53701

Phone: (608) 833-5952
Fax: (608) 833-5990
Telex 9102404210 MIDAG MSN UQ
Cables: MIDAG

Contact: Donald A. Viereg, President

Year Established: 1952
Geographic specialization: Caribbean, Middle &
Far East

Provides EMC services for:
farm equipment and products; food
processing/packaging machinery and equipment;
machinery and supplies.

Midwest Enterprises
8493 16th Road
Almond, WI 54909

Phone: (715) 366-8800
Fax: (715) 366-4400

Contact: Mark Dzulynsky, President
Year Established: 1987

Geographic specialization: Worldwide

Provides EMC services for:
aircraft, accessories or parts; building materials;
chemicals, chemical and petrochemical industries
equipment and products; general commodities.

EXPORT CONSULTANTS

Export management companies often serve as export consultants to industries and companies. Yet, there are many other knowledgeable consultants who consult on some aspect of exporting but who cannot be defined as an EMC.

These consultants serve a wide variety of company needs. They can help set up an export department, determine if a product is exportable, or set up distribution channels. Sometimes an export consultant is called upon to crack an unusual market (the Turkish video market, for example), or to woo a particularly difficult industry, like telecommunications.

If the shipping of your product is highly regulated (explosives, defense electronics, etc.), consider hiring an export consultant with expertise in this field. If you ned to train staff members on export licensing requirements, there are consultants who do this.

Most of these consultants work on a fee-only basis, although some do consider commissions or other incentives if they are working on consulting for the sales and marketing departments.

Beginning on page 111 is a list of export consultants we've encountered while doing research for this *Directory.* Please note that some EMCs in the previous section are also cited as providing consulting services.

Tratech International, Inc.
2100 First Ave. North, Suite 500
Birmingham, AL 35203

Phone: (205) 324-8200
Fax: (205) 324-8822

Contact: Donald R. Cowsar, President
Year Established: 1988

Geographic specialization: Europe, Japan

Provides EMC services for:
chemicals, chemical and petrochemical industries equipment and products; medical equipment; optical, photographic, and scientific instruments; pharmaceuticals and hospital supplies. Intellectual property consultants.

American Amenities, Inc.
500 Airport Blvd., Suite 229
Burlingame, CA 94010

Phone: (415) 375-0207
Fax: (415) 375-0726

Contact: Hiroshi Higashijima, President
Year Established: 1988

Foreign language capabilities: Japanese
Geographic specialization: Japan

Provides EMC services for:
building materials; consumer service industries: specialized machinery and equipment; furniture; hardware; heating, air-conditioning and refrigeration; household furnishings and appliances; lighting; medical equipment; paints, varnishes and enamels; restaurant, hotel and catering equipment; safety and security equipment; sporting goods. Specializes in architectural designs and computer software.

Frontier Trading
12555 Oaks North Dr., Suite 205
Rancho Bernardo, CA 92128

Phone: (619) 485-8867
Fax: (706) 637-5028

Contact: Martin J. Capdevilla, President
Year Established: 1988

Foreign language capabilities: Spanish
Geographic specialization: Mexico

Provides EMC services for:
food products and beverages; games, toys, etc.; safety and security equipment; cosmetics and toiletries. Provides broker/distributor services.

International ICS Group Inc.
P. O. Box 4082
Irvine, CA 92716

Phone: (714) 552-9494
Contact: R. A. Jamess, Vice President

Year Established: 1946
Geographic specialization: Europe, Austral/Asia, Middle East, Latin America

Provides EMC services for:
apparel, textiles, garment components and leather goods; audio-visual equipment and educational/training aids; chemicals, chemical and petrochemical industries equipment and products; electrical, radio and TV, equipment and parts; games, toys, etc.; household furnishings and appliances; machinery and supplies; medical equipment; marine and related products; sporting goods; lubricants.

International Information Specialists
2352 Santa Anita Dr.
Sacramento, CA 95825

Phone: (916) 488-3523
Contact: John E. Hawes, President

Year Established: 1984
Foreign language capabilities: German, Russian

Geographic specialization: Europe

Provides EMC services for:
communication equipment and systems; computers, peripherals, business equipment and software; construction equipment; consumer service industries: specialized machinery and equipment; electrical, radio and TV, equipment and parts.

International Trades
9459 Maler Rd.
San Diego, CA 92129

Phone: (619) 538-0423
Fax: (619) 538-0788
Telex 4973174 HAJ

Contact: Sam Hajjiri, President
Year Established: 1986

Foreign language capabilities: Arabic, Spanish, French, Italian, German, Farsi
Geographic specialization: Europe, Far East, Middle East, South & Latin America, Africa

Provides EMC services for:
accessories, luggage and jewelry; aircraft, accessories or parts; audio-visual equipment and educational/training aids; chemicals, chemical and petrochemical industries equipment and products; furniture; gasolines, lubricants, and equipment; graphic arts, printing equipment and supplies; hardware; industrial products and equipment; marine and related products; paper, packaging and containers; safety and security equipment. Handles all types of products. Worldwide import-export consultants.

ITM Corporation
1815 W. 213th St., Suite 200
Torrance, CA 90501

Phone: (213) 328-9021
Fax: (213) 328-9164

Contact: Steve Feinberg, President

Foreign language capabilities: Japanese
Geographic specialization: Japan and Pacific Rim

Provides EMC services for:
aircraft, accessories or parts; apparel, textiles, garment components, leather goods; audio-visual equip. and educational/training aids; automobiles, accessories or parts; communication equip. and systems; computers, peripherals, business equip., software; construction equip.; electrical, radio and TV, equip. and parts; farm equip. and products; food products and beverages; games, toys; medical equip.; paper, packaging and containers; pharmaceuticals and hospital supplies; restaurant, hotel and catering equip.; safety and security equip.; sporting goods; trucks, accessories or parts; entertainment industry products & services. Provides trade and marketing mgmt. co. services.

Morse Agri-Energy Associates
220 Montgomery St., Suite 432
San Francisco, CA 95104-3410

Phone: (415) 391-7501
Fax: (415) 391-7537

Contact: Scott D. Morse, President
Year Established: 1971

Foreign language capabilities: French
Geographic specialization: Worldwide

Provides EMC services for:
air and water purification, pollution control and environmental control products and equipment; farm equipment and products; food processing/packaging machinery and equipment; food products and beverages; mining equipment, minerals and raw materials; paper, packaging and containers; agricultural commodities.

Smythe International Services
1610 La Pradera Dr., Suite 15
Campbell, CA 95008

Phone: (408) 374-3580
Fax: (408) 374-6199

Contact: Jeanne H. Smythe, President
Year Established: 1984

Geographic specialization: Worldwide

Provides EMC services for:
communication equipment and systems; computers, peripherals, business equipment and software; consumer service industries: specialized machinery and equipment; games, toys, etc.; hardware; industrial products and equipment; medical equipment; testing equipment.

Trade Pacific International
310 Walker St.
Watsonville, CA 95076

Phone: (408) 724-6000
Fax: (408) 728-5708
Telex 171538

Contact: Lisa A. Haas, Trade Specialist
Year Established: 1984

Geographic specialization: Canada, Europe, Pacific Rim

Consultants International, Ltd.
161 Washington Ave.
Bridgeport, CT 06604

Phone: (203) 226-2725
Fax: (203) 221-0825

Contact: J. Lynn Helms, Chairman
Year Established: 1984

Geographic specialization: Western & Eastern Europe, China, Australia, South America

Rusk International Corp.
11 Stone Drive
Westport, CT 06880

Phone: (203) 227-7721

Contact: Milton L. Rusk, President
Year Established: 1974

Foreign language capabilities: French
Geographic specialization: Europe, Japan

Schneider-Sohn & Associates, Inc.
P. O. Box 5237
Westport, CT 06881

Phone: (203) 454-2147
Fax: (203) 227-9590
Telex 510-6006651

Contact: Stephen Sohn, President
Year Established: 1986

Foreign language capabilities: French, German
Geographic specialization: Worldwide

Provides EMC services for:
aircraft, accessories or parts.

High Technology Export Services, Inc.
1100 Connecticut Ave., N.W., Suite 535
Washington, DC 20036

Phone: (202) 775-8781
Fax: (202) 862-4996

Contact: James Sell, President
Year Established: 1987

Foreign language capabilities: Japanese
Geographic specialization: Worldwide

Provides EMC services for:
aircraft, accessories or parts; chemicals, chemical and petrochemical industries equipment and products; communication equipment and systems; computers, peripherals, business equipment and software; electrical, radio and TV, equipment and parts; industrial products and equipment; marine and related products; optical, photographic, and scientific instruments; testing equipment; munitions.

MK Technology/Deltac
1920 N Street, Suite 600
Washington, DC 20036

Phone: (202) 463-0904
Fax: (202) 429-9812

Contact: Glen D. Schroeder, Vice President, Marketing
Year Established: 1985

Foreign language capabilities: German, French, Spanish, Japanese
Geographic specialization: USSR, Japan, Israel, E & W Europe

Provides EMC services for:
aircraft, accessories or parts; communication equipment and systems; computers, peripherals, business equipment and software; consumer service industries: specialized machinery and equipment; mining equipment, minerals and raw materials; optical, photographic, and scientific instruments; testing equipment. Provides consulting services re. export licenses for national security controlled items.

Provides EMC services for:
food products and beverages.

Provides EMC services for:
aircraft, accessories or parts; communication equipment and systems; high/advanced technology products; air traffic controls.

Provides EMC services for:
accessories, luggage and jewelry; apparel, textiles, garment components and leather goods; food processing/packaging machinery and equipment; industrial products and equipment; medical equipment; paper, packaging and containers; testing equipment.

International Business Resources, Inc.
900 Fort St., Suite 1777
Honolulu, HI 96813

Phone: (808) 521-8204
Fax: (808) 536-7646

Contact: Dennis T. Oshiro, President
Year Established: 1982

Foreign language capabilities: Japanese
Geographic specialization: Japan, Asia-Pacific region

Provides EMC services for:
air and water purification, pollution control and environmental control products and equipment; aircraft, accessories or parts; audio-visual equipment and educational/training aids; computers, peripherals, business equipment and software; medical equipment; marine and related products; optical, photographic, and scientific instruments; pharmaceuticals and hospital supplies.

Raba Corporation
1144 Hunakai St.
Honolulu, HI 96816-4613

Phone: (808) 735-1357
Fax: (808) 735-1357
Telex 705 7430333 RABACORP

Contact: Rafael Aberin, President
Year Established: 1981

Foreign language capabilities: Japanese, Spanish, German, French
Geographic specialization: Worldwide

Provides EMC services for:
aircraft, accessories or parts; apparel, textiles, garment components and leather goods; chemicals, chemical and petrochemical industries equipment and products; electrical, radio and TV, equipment and parts; farm equipment and products; food processing/packaging machinery and equipment; food products and beverages; machinery and supplies; pharmaceuticals and hospital supplies.

Alkier Consulting (Consult U.S.A., Inc.)
2431 W. Irving Park Rd.
Chicago, IL 60618

Phone: (312) 583-2514
Fax: (312) 583-8807

Contact: Wolfgang M. Alkier, President
Year Established: 1984

Foreign language capabilities: German, French
Geographic specialization: Europe

Provides EMC services for:
apparel, textiles, garment components and leather goods; automobiles, accessories or parts; communication equipment and systems; computers, peripherals, business equipment and software; farm equipment and products; food products and beverages; furniture; games, toys, etc.; heating, air-conditioning and refrigeration; machinery and supplies; medical equipment; restaurant, hotel and catering equipment; sporting goods.

Chicago Import/Export Consultants
1350 W. Lake St., Suite 1F
Roselle, IL 60172

Phone: (708) 307-7011
Fax: (708) 307-7022
Telex 284683 BERT UR

Contact: Edward G. Bertram, President
Year Established: 1985

Foreign language capabilities: Mandarin
Geographic specialization: Asia, Far East, Pacific Rim

Provides EMC services for:
air and water purification, pollution control and environmental control products and equipment; automobiles, accessories or parts; chemicals, chemical and petrochemical industries equipment and products; food processing/packaging machinery and equipment; food products and beverages; gasolines, lubricants, and equipment; industrial products and equipment; optical, photographic, and scientific instruments; testing equipment; trucks, accessories or parts; precision metal products. Provides real estate investment consulting services.

Fremont Group Limited
175 N. Franklin St., Suite 302
Chicago, IL 60613

Phone: (312) 332-4096
Fax: (312) 263-2549
Telex 256698 FGL UR

Contact: Larry J. Marshaus, Vice President
Year Established: 1983

Geographic specialization: Southeast Asia, India, Pakistan, Malaysia

Provides EMC services for:
air and water purification, pollution control and environmental control products and equipment; aircraft, accessories or parts; apparel, textiles, garment components and leather goods; consumer service industries: specialized machinery and equipment; farm equipment and products; food products and beverages; medical equipment; materials handling equipment. Provides international business development and consulting services.

Levinson, Samuel & Associates, Inc.
182 Maple Hill Rd.
Glencoe, IL 60022

Phone: (708) 835-0182
Fax: (708) 835-5141
Telex 350195

Contact: Samuel Levinson, Chairman
Year Established: 1973

Geographic specialization: India

Provides EMC services for:
air and water purification, pollution control and environmental control products and equipment; automobiles, accessories or parts; building materials; chemicals, chemical and petrochemical industries equipment and products; communication equipment and systems; computers, peripherals, business equipment and software; construction equipment; consumer service industries: specialized machinery and equipment; food products and beverages; graphic arts, printing equipment and supplies; industrial products and equipment; machinery and supplies; sporting goods. Provides services re. collaborative ventures.

Trans Tech Management Consulting, Ltd.
601 Skokie Blvd.
Northbrook, IL 60062

Phone: (708) 480-7878
Fax: (708) 480-9174
Telex (WUI) 323465 TRANSTECH CGO

Contact: Lawrence H. Rubly, Managing Partner
Year Established: 1981

Foreign language capabilities: German, Russian, Spanish, Chinese, Arabic
Geographic specialization: Europe, Latin America, Middle East, China

Provides EMC services for:
apparel, textiles, garment components and leather goods; building materials; graphic arts, printing equipment and supplies; hardware; lighting; medical equipment.

International Communications, Inc.
46 Washington St.
Natick, MA 01760

Phone: (508) 651-9232
Fax: (508) 653-9183

Contact: Roger Jeanty, President
Year Established: 1984

Foreign language capabilities: French, Spanish, German, Italian, Japanese
Geographic specialization: Europe, Far East

Provides EMC services for:
communication equipment and systems; computers, peripherals, business equipment and software; hardware; industrial products and equipment. Provides translation services.

Marketshare Inc.
21 Cochituate Rd.
Wayland, MA 01778

Phone: (508) 358-2154
Fax: (508) 358-6350

Contact: James H. Geisman, President
Year Established: 1982

Foreign language capabilities: Japanese
Geographic specialization: Japan

Provides EMC services for:
communication equipment and systems; computers, peripherals, business equipment and software; electrical, radio and TV, equipment and parts.

H. L. International Trade Advisors
3403 Lyndale Ave. South
Minneapolis, MN 55408

Phone: (612) 824-7931
Fax: (612) 824-7945

Contact: Gerald R. Lee, Vice President
Year Established: 1987

Geographic specialization: Western Europe, Far East

Provides EMC services for:
automobiles, accessories or parts; machinery and supplies.

British-American Forfaiting Co., Inc.
7700 Clayton Rd., Suite 306
St. Louis, MO 63117

Phone: (314) 647-8700
Fax: (314) 647-7943

Contact: David W. McGhee, President
Year Established: 1988

Foreign language capabilities: Spanish, German
Geographic specialization: Third World

Provides EMC services for:
aircraft, accessories or parts; automobiles, accessories or parts; chemicals, chemical and petrochemical industries equipment and products; consumer service industries: specialized machinery and equipment; gasolines, lubricants, and equipment; industrial products and equipment; machinery and supplies; materials handling equipment; mining equipment, minerals and raw materials. Provides trade finance consulting services for a wide variety of products.

Interconsult
Box 880
North Hampton, NH 03862

Phone: (603) 964-6464
Fax: (603) 964-9747
Telex 650 325 1373

Contact: Jo-Anne L. Funke, Managing Partner
Year Established: 1978

Geographic specialization: Europe

Provides EMC services for:
computers, peripherals, business equipment and software.

AmTrade Aid, Inc.
25 Manor Dr., Suite 14-J
Newark, NJ 07106

Phone: (201) 371-5112
Fax: (201) 399-7025
Telex 650-376-4897

Contact: Dr. Boris Povlotsky, Director
Year Established: 1988

Foreign language capabilities: Russian, Bulgarian, Czechoslovakian, Polish, Hungarian
Geographic specialization: USSR, Eastern Europe

Provides EMC services for:
air and water purification, pollution control and environmental control products and equip.; apparel, textiles, garment components and leather goods; chemicals, chemical and petrochemical industries equip. and products; communication equip. and systems; computers, peripherals, business equip. and software; construction equip.; consumer service industries: specialized machinery and equipment; electrical, radio and TV, equip. and parts; food processing/packaging machinery and equip.; heating, A/C and refrigeration; industrial products and equip.; materials handling equip.; mining equip., minerals and raw materials.

Fay, John J.
120 Iroquois Ave.
Lake Hiawatha, NJ 07034

Phone: (201) 335-8814

Contact: John J. Fay, President
Year Established: 1987

Foreign language capabilities: Korean
Geographic specialization: Far East

Provides   consulting services.

Intertrade Services, Inc.
307 Evers St.
Wyckoff, NJ 07481

Phone: (201) 652-7335
Fax: (201) 445-5485

Contact: Thomas L. Aman, President
Year Established: 1986

Foreign language capabilities: Russian
Geographic specialization: USSR, Eastern Europe

Provides EMC services for:
aircraft, accessories or parts; apparel, textiles, garment components and leather goods; audio-visual equip. and educational/training aids; automobiles, accessories or parts; building materials; chemicals, chemical and petrochemical industries equip. and products; communication equip. and systems; computers, peripherals, business equip. and software; construction equip.; electrical, radio and TV, equip. and parts; gasolines, lubricants, and equip.; medical equip.; mining equip., minerals and raw materials. Provides financial services consulting.
SEE ADVERTISEMENT, PAGE 115.

Items Unlimited
132-1 Route 522
Jamesburg, NJ 08831

Phone: (201) 521-2436
Fax: (201) 521-1667

Contact: Joseph R. Scranton, President

Year Established: 1990
Geographic specialization: Asia, Europe, Mexico

Provides EMC services for:
apparel, textiles, garment components and leather goods; communication equipment and systems; marine and related products; sporting goods; prefabricated housing and log homes; general merchandise. Provides international market research services.

Kallman Associates

5 Maple Court
Ridgewood, NJ 07450

Phone: (201) 652-7070
Fax: (201) 652-3898

Contact: Tom Kallman, Manager
Year Established: 1960

Foreign language capabilities: German
Geographic specialization: Europe, especially Germany

Provides EMC services for:
accessories, luggage and jewelry; aircraft, accessories or parts; apparel, textiles, garment components and leather goods; building materials; communication equipment and systems; computers, peripherals, business equipment and software; food products and beverages; heating, air-conditioning and refrigeration; materials handling equipment; mining equipment, minerals and raw materials; restaurant, hotel and catering equipment; defense industry, airport and ground support equipment. Trade show organizers.

Alpha Int'l Management Group, Ltd.

145 West 58th St.
New York, NY 10019

Phone: (212) 956-2200
Fax: (212) 247-4420

Contact: Marc M. Sussman, President

Foreign language capabilities: Spanish, French, Italian
Geographic specialization: Europe

Provides market entry strategies.

EEC Resources

P.O. Box 1951
New York, NY 10004

Phone: (516) 432-4728
Fax: (516) 549-6996

Contact: Joel Weiss, President

Year Established: 1986
Geographic specialization: E & W Europe, Middle East

International transportation and lease financing consultants.

Heemsoth-Kerner Corp.

7 Dey St.
New York, NY 10007

Phone: (212) 608-9755
Fax: (212) 349-4434
Telex WU 64-9057   *Cables:* HEMSOBAS

Contact: Robert M. Cahill, Vice President, Export
Year Established: 1920

Geographic specialization: Worldwide

Export/import shipping consultants.

SEE ADVERTISEMENT, PAGE 113.

Syntra Ltd.

505 Eighth Ave., 15th Fl.
New York, NY 10018-6505

Phone: (212) 714-0440
Fax: (212) 967-4623

Contact: Dano T. Anthos
Year Established: 1984

Provides computer software for the exporting industry.

Kimain Co.

P.O. Box 81
Wickliffe, OH 44092

Phone: (216) 289-4222
Fax: (216) 289-4222

Contact: Casimir Kacperski, President
Year Established: 1984

Foreign language capabilities: Japanese
Geographic specialization: Far East

Provides EMC services for:
accessories, luggage and jewelry; apparel, textiles, garment components and leather goods; industrial products and equipment; machinery and supplies; sporting goods. Provides finder services.

Kip Company, The
1925 Lakeview Ave.
Cleveland, OH 44116-2413

Phone: (216) 331-8974
Fax: (216) 333-5473
Telex 298233 KIPCO UR

Contact: Nancy J. Kuder, Distribution
Year Established: 1983

Geographic specialization: Worldwide

Provides EMC services for:
chemicals, chemical and petrochemical industries equipment and products.

OREXPO Services, Inc.
P. O. Box 19570
Portland, OR 97219

Phone: (503) 244-9113
Fax: (503) 244-0576

Contact: Lisa A. Frenz, Vice President, Operations
Year Established: 1982

Foreign language capabilities: Spanish, German
Geographic specialization: Far East, Europe

Consultants in international trade for small and medium sized manufacturers.

Turnkey Projects, Inc.
P. O. Box 1128
Portland, OR 97207

Phone: (503) 244-9824
Fax: (503) 244-6541
Telex 4947420 (TPI UI)

Contact: James W. Hanna, Managing Director
Year Established: 1982

Foreign language capabilities: Arabic
Geographic specialization: Caribbean, Pacific Rim, Europe, Middle East

Provides EMC services for:
apparel, textiles, garment components and leather goods; building materials; consumer service industries: specialized machinery and equipment; food products and beverages; machinery and supplies.

Swartz, Anthony M. & Associates, Inc.
18 Sentry Parkway, Suite 1
Blue Bell, PA 19422

Phone: (215) 549-2295
Fax: (215) 540-2290
Cables: "EXDEP"/Philadelphia, PA

Contact: Anthony M. Swartz, President
Year Established: 1976

Foreign language capabilities: Spanish, Portuguese
Geographic specialization: Caribbean, Latin America, Pacific Rim, Europe, Middle East

Consultants on specialized projects.

International Enterprises
P. O. Box 240113
Memphis, TN 38124-0113

Phone: (901) 683-3575

Contact: Bradford H. Rice, President
Year Established: 1985

Geographic specialization: Middle East, Southeast Asia, Japan, Australia, Canada

Provides EMC services for:
building materials; gasolines, lubricants, and equipment; medical equipment; pharmaceuticals and hospital supplies; restaurant, hotel and catering equipment; railroad locomotive parts and accessories.

Global Dimensions Corp.
1015 Francis Dr.
College Station TX 77840

Phone: (409) 693-9940
Fax: (409) 693-0603
Telex ITT 44901119MUR

Contact: Kelly J. Murphrey, Vice President
Year Established: 1988

Foreign language capabilities: Spanish
Geographic specialization: Latin America, Europe, Africa

Provides EMC services for:
audio-visual equipment and educational/training aids; chemicals, chemical and petrochemical industries equipment and products; farm equipment and products; medical equipment; pharmaceuticals and hospital supplies.

SPC International
1500 Wilson Blvd.
Arlington, VA 22209-2454

Phone: (703) 841-2800
Fax: (703) 527-6037
Cables: TWX (710) 955-0678

Contact: Richard N. Smull, Director
Year Established: 1970

Provides defense-related consulting services.

Mancor
P. O. Box 1865
Bellevue, WA 98009

Phone: (206) 885-1051
Fax: (206) 885-1156
Telex 221451 MCOR UR   *Cables:* MANRING

Contact: A. B. Manring, President
Year Established: 1971

Foreign language capabilities: French, Chinese
Geographic specialization: Developing countries world-wide

Provides EMC services for:
audio-visual equipment and educational/training aids; computers, peripherals, business equipment and software; farm equipment and products; food processing/packaging machinery and equipment; machinery and supplies; optical, photographic, and scientific instruments; testing equipment. Provides procurement services.

PRODUCT CATEGORIES

The index on the following pages is divided into the 41 product categories listed below. Each category index lists, alphabetically, the EMCs and consultants which handle the products in that category, the state in which they are located, and the page number in this book containing their complete listing.

Automobile International   •   *Industrial World*   •   *Export*   •   *High Technology Export & Import*

1. ACCESSORIES, LUGGAGE & JEWELRY

Asia Marketing & Consulting Corp.	UT	105	Kallman Associates	NJ	117
Aztek International Corp.	IN	38	Kammeh Int'l Trade Co.	IL	35
Ballagh & Thrall, Inc.	PA	98	Kimain Co.	OH	117
Beijing Trade Exchange, Inc.	DC	21	Midwestern Trading Corp.	IL	36
C. International	NJ	54	New Mexico Int'l Trade & Devel. Co.	NM	62
Celestial Mercantile Corp.	NY	68	Niconor International Corporation	CA	11
Comanache Moon Trading Co.	TX	103	Pacific Export Services, Inc.	TX	105
Comtrade International Inc.	NY	70	Proxima Inc.	NY	84
EX-IM U.S.A., Inc.	IL	33	Rizzo, Joseph F. Company	AZ	1
Expotech	GA	30	Roldan Products Corporation	MO	50
General Product Co., Inc.	NJ	57	Romac Export Management Corp.	CA	14
Globelink Incorporated	TX	104	Rusk International Corp.	CT	112
Grand Pacific Finance Corp.	NY	74	TRADECO Association of N.Y., Ltd.	NY	87
IFRAS, Inc.	NY	77	Universial Export Agencies	NY	88
International Trades	CA	111	UTAC America Inc.	NY	88
Intra-World Export Co., Inc.	NY	78			

2. AIR & WATER PURIFICATION, POLLUTION CONTROL & ENVIRONMENTAL CONTROL

A & S International Marketing Co., Inc.	NY	64	Fremont Group Limited	IL	114
Actrade International Corp.	NY	64	Gas International Corp., The	NJ	57
Ad. Auriema Inc.	NY	66	Geonex International Corp.	NY	74
Allied Systems Export Corp.	PA	97	Gerber, J. & Co., Inc.	NY	74
AME Matex Corp.	NJ	54	Glynn International, Inc.	MA	46
American Eagle Purchasing Agents	MA	44	Grable, John Exports, Inc.	FL	25
American Industrial Export Ltd.	NY	66	Haller, Mart Inc.	FL	26
AmTrade Aid, Inc.	NJ	116	HCI Corporation	VA	106
Anaheim Marketing International	CA	3	Hockman Lewis Limited	NJ	57
ARC International Group, Inc.	MA	45	Inter Euro Trading, Inc.	NY	78
Aztek International Corp.	IN	38	Intercontinental Enterprises Ltd.	CA	9
Bauer, Alex & Co.	NJ	54	International Business Resources, Inc.	HI	114
Berkowitz, N. C. & Company	CA	4	International Controls Co., Inc.	PA	100
Boar's Head Int'l Trading Co.	WA	106	International Marketing Services Co.	WA	107
Browne International Industries, Inc.	NY	68	Jahn, Henry R. & Son, Inc.	NY	78
Chicago Import/Export Consultants	IL	114	Jajin Trading and Marketing, Inc.	WA	107
Continental Enterprises	CA	5	JDRAS Enterprises, Inc.	NJ	58
Davis Elliott International Inc.	PA	98	Kammeh Int'l Trade Co.	IL	35
Debco Chemicals Sales, Co.	NY	70	Levinson, Samuel & Associates, Inc.	IL	114
Domestic & International Technology	PA	98	M International Export (MINTEX)	VA	106
Donovan, W. J. Co.	NY	70	Mercator Corporation	PA	101
Eagle International Enterprises, Inc.	CA	5	Morse Agri-Energy Associates	CA	112
Engineering Equipment Co.	IL	33	Natcom International	OH	94
Euroscand, Inc.	FL	24	Nikiforov, George, Inc.	NY	83
Expomar International Inc.	NJ	56	Orbis International, Ltd.	CA	12
Export Consultant Service	PA	98	Overseas Services Corp.	IL	36
Fame International	TX	103	Pegasus International Corp.	NJ	60
Ferrex International, Inc.	NY	72	Prestige U.S. Exports	FL	27

Rajiv International, Inc.	MD	44	Tecnomasters International Corp.	NY	86
Rebel, Albert & Associates, Inc.	CA	14	TRADECO Association of N.Y., Ltd.	NY	87
Regalis USA, Inc.	CA	14	United Exporters Service, Inc.	KY	41
RKF International Inc.	IL	37	UTAC America Inc.	NY	88
Semsco International	FL	28	Verde America, Inc.	NY	90
Sharoubim International Group, Inc.	NY	84	Wellesley International Corp.	MA	47
Strato Enterprises	NJ	61	Witz Scientific, Inc.	OH	96
Subent Co., Inc.	IL	38	Worldwide Exporters, Inc.	CA	18
Surel International, Inc.	MA	47	Worldwide Trade Opportunities, Inc.	CA	18
Sylvan Ginsbury Ltd.	NJ	61	XPORT, Port Authority Trading Co.	NY	91
Technic Group	TN	103	ZED Group, Inc.	MA	47

3. AIRCRAFT, ACCESSORIES OR PARTS

A & S International Marketing Co., Inc.	NY	64	Kallman Associates	NJ	117
Actrade International Corp.	NY	64	Kellogg International, Inc.	IL	35
Amerasia Trading Co., Inc.	CA	2	Latco International, Inc.	SC	102
American Export Trading Co.	CA	2	M International Export (MINTEX)	VA	106
Asia Marketing & Consulting Corp.	UT	105	Midwest Enterprises	WI	109
Automotive International Corp.	TX	103	Midwestern Trading Corp.	IL	36
Avalon Group, Ltd.	CA	4	MK Technology/Deltac	DC	113
Berkowitz, N. C. & Company	CA	4	Natcom International	OH	94
British-American Forfaiting Co., Inc.	MO	116	New Mexico Int'l Trade & Devel. Co.	NM	62
C.C.I., Inc.	IL	32	Pierce International	CA	13
Chazen Industrial Corp.	NJ	55	Quatro International, Inc.	FL	28
Consultants International, Ltd.	CT	112	Raba Corporation	HI	114
CPS Marketing Corp.	FL	23	RKF International Inc.	IL	37
Debco Chemicals Sales, Co.	NY	70	Rodriguez, R.A., Inc.	NY	84
Eagle International Enterprises, Inc.	CA	5	Schneider-Sohn & Associates, Inc.	CT	113
EMB Trading Co.	NY	72	Sharoubim International Group, Inc.	NY	84
Empire Equities Inc.	NY	72	Silo International, Inc.	NY	86
Ewig, Carl F. Inc.	NJ	56	Sosin International, Inc.	GA	30
Fremont Group Limited	IL	114	Spivey, James S., Inc.	MD	44
Gladex Corporation	CA	6	Strato Enterprises	NJ	61
Globelink Incorporated	TX	104	Sylvan Ginsbury Ltd.	NJ	61
Hemisol Export & Import Corp.	FL	26	Technic Group	TN	103
High Technology Export Services, Inc.	DC	113	Timcorp Int'l Marketing Co., Ltd.	HI	31
International Business Resources,	HI	114	Torning International, Inc.	CT	20
International Trades	CA	111	Trade Development Corp. of Chicago	CA	16
Intertech Worldwide Corp.	FL	26	Tradex International, Inc.	CA	17
Intertrade Services, Inc.	NJ	116	United Gulf Services, Inc.	CA	17
ITBR, Inc.	TX	104	VIE International Inc.	CT	20
ITM Corporation	CA	112	Wellesley International Corp.	MA	47
Kalamazoo International, Inc.	MI	48	Wolfson, P. J. Co., Inc.	NY	91

4. APPAREL, TEXTILES, GARMENT COMPONENTS & LEATHER GOODS

Abaco International Corp.	CA	2	ARC International Group, Inc.	MA	45
Alkier Consulting (Consult U.S.A., Inc.)	IL	114	Ballagh & Thrall, Inc.	PA	98
AmTrade Aid, Inc.	NJ	116	Beijing Trade Exchange, Inc.	DC	21

Bogart International Sales	OH	92	McLean International Marketing, Inc.	WI	108
C. International	NJ	54	Muni Trading Co., Inc.	NJ	60
Celestial Mercantile Corp.	NY	68	Natcom International	OH	94
Colonial International Corp.- COINCO	FL	23	New Mexico Int'l Trade & Devel. Co.	NM	62
Comanache Moon Trading Co.	TX	103	New World Management, Inc.	NY	82
Comtrade International Inc.	NY	70	Niconor International Corporation	CA	11
Embree, C. A. Co.	TN	102	Pacific Export Services, Inc.	TX	105
Ewig, Carl F. Inc.	NJ	56	Piedmont Caribbean Trade Limited	NC	52
Export Trade of America, Inc.	NY	72	Proxima Inc.	NY	84
Fernandez Import/Export, Inc. USA	NC	50	Quatro International, Inc.	FL	28
Fremont Group Limited	IL	114	Raba Corporation	HI	114
Global Merchandising Corp.	CA	6	RHA Group	CA	14
IFRAS, Inc.	NY	77	RKF International Inc.	IL	37
INSECO, Inc.	NY	77	Roldan Products Corporation	MO	50
Inter Euro Trading, Inc.	NY	78	Romac Export Management Corp.	CA	14
International ICS Group Inc.	CA	111	Rusk International Corp.	CT	112
International Industries Corp.	SC	102	TRADECO Association of N.Y., Ltd.	NY	87
International Product Mktg. Group Inc.	CA	9	Trans Tech Management Consulting,	IL	115
Intertrade Services, Inc.	NJ	116	Turnkey Projects, Inc.	OR	118
Intra-World Export Co., Inc.	NY	78	Universial Export Agencies	NY	88
Items Unlimited	NJ	116	USExport, Inc.	NY	88
ITM Corporation	CA	112	UTAC America Inc.	NY	88
Jajin Trading and Marketing, Inc.	WA	107	Verde America, Inc.	NY	90
Kallman Associates	NJ	117	VIE International Inc.	CT	20
Kammeh Int'l Trade Co.	IL	35	World-Trade Services, Inc.	OH	96
Kato International, Inc.	NJ	58	Worldwide Trade Opportunities, Inc.	CA	18
Kimain Co.	OH	117	XPORT, Port Authority Trading Co.	NY	91
Lotus Group, The	NC	52			

5. AUDIO-VISUAL EQUIPMENT; EDUCATIONAL TRAINING AIDS

A & S International Marketing Co., Inc.	NY	64	ITM Corporation	CA	112
Amas International, Inc.	FL	22	JDRAS Enterprises, Inc.	NJ	58
Beijing Trade Exchange, Inc.	DC	21	Kato International, Inc.	NJ	58
Camex International, Inc.	FL	23	Mancor	WA	119
Global Dimensions Corp.	TX	118	Meridian Synapse Corp.	NY	81
Global Marketing Concepts	NC	52	Midwestern Trading Corp.	IL	36
Global Technology, Inc.	CA	6	Ohio Overseas Corporation	OH	94
Globelink Incorporated	TX	104	Onyx Enterprises, Inc.	NY	83
Glynn International, Inc.	MA	46	Pacific Export Services, Inc.	TX	105
IMEX Trading, Ltd.	CA	8	Prestige U.S. Exports	FL	27
Import Export Management Svc., Inc.	TX	104	Quest International	HI	31
International Business Resources,	HI	114	RKF International Inc.	IL	37
International Consolidated Exchange	OH	93	Sacks, Harvey C. Export Consulting	CA	15
International ICS Group Inc.	CA	111	Surel International, Inc.	MA	47
International Trades	CA	111	Technic Group	TN	103
Intertrade Services, Inc.	NJ	116	Tradeways, Ltd.	VA	106
ITBR, Inc.	TX	104	Wolfson, P. J. Co., Inc.	NY	91

6. AUTOMOBILES, ACCESSORIES OR PARTS

Abaco International Corp.	CA	2
Acarex, Inc.	NY	64
Ajax International Corp.	FL	21
Alkier Consulting (Consult U.S.A., Inc.)	IL	114
American Export Trading Co.	CA	2
American International Pacific	CA	3
American Trade International Corp.	UT	105
Amsco-Valley Forge	NY	66
Amtrade International Corp.	CA	3
Asia Marketing & Consulting Corp.	UT	105
Asia Minor Export Import Co., Inc.	NJ	54
Atlantech Inc.	FL	22
Atlas Asia-Pacific	CA	3
Automotive Export Inc.	FL	22
Automotive International Corp.	TX	103
Aztek International Corp.	IN	38
Bisho, J. R. Co., Inc.	CA	4
Bock Pharmaceutical, Inc.	OH	92
British-American Forfaiting Co., Inc.	MO	116
C.C.I., Inc.	IL	32
Caravan Export Corp.	NY	68
Celestial Mercantile Corp.	NY	68
Charon-Jessam Trading Co. Inc.	NY	69
Chazen Industrial Corp.	NJ	55
Chicago Import/Export Consultants	IL	114
Colonial International Corp.- COINCO	FL	23
Crown Automotive Sales Co., Inc.	MA	45
Da Miano & Graham Ltd.	IL	32
Davis Elliott International Inc.	PA	98
Detroit Parts Mfg. Co.	MI	48
Domestic & International Technology	PA	98
Drake America	NY	71
Dreyco, Inc.	NJ	55
Dreyfus & Associates, Ltd.	NY	71
Dunlap Export Co., Inc.	OH	92
Duromotive Industries, Inc.	NY	71
Eagle International Enterprises, Inc.	CA	5
Engineering Equipment Co.	IL	33
ERW International Inc.	IL	33
EX-IM U.S.A., Inc.	IL	33
Exmart International, Inc.	NJ	56
Export Agencies Int'l Corp.	IN	39
Expotech	GA	30
Express Parts	OH	93
Fernandez Import/Export, Inc. USA	NC	50
Fields International	IL	33
Fischer Enterprises Inc.	NY	73
FMI Automotive Corp./FMI Trading	NY	73
Geon International Corp.	IN	39
Gerson International Corp.	IN	39
Global Marketing Services, Inc.	FL	25
Global Merchandising Corp.	CA	6
Gomez, Manuel and Associates, Inc.	FL	25
H. L. Int'l Trade Advisors	MN	115
Handforth Company, The	PA	100
Hayden, Inc.	CA	7
Hemisol Export & Import Corp.	FL	26
Hosler & Associates, Inc.	MO	50
IBEX Technical Corp.	PA	100
IFRAS, Inc.	NY	77
IMEX Trading, Ltd.	CA	8
Indamerica International, Inc.	CA	8
Industrial Engineering Int'l, Inc.	IL	34
INSECO, Inc.	NY	77
International Industries Corp.	SC	102
International Product Mktg. Group Inc.	CA	9
Intertrade Services, Inc.	NJ	116
Intertrade, Inc.	MI	48
Intraco Corporation	MI	48
Intrade Inc.	OH	94
Iowa Export Import Trading Co.	IA	41
ISIS International Export Mgmt. Co.	UT	105
ITM Corporation	CA	112
J & M Company, Ltd.	IL	35
J & M Sales Corporation	NJ	58
Kalamazoo International, Inc.	MI	48
Karl, Peter A., International Sales	NY	79
Levinson, Samuel & Associates, Inc.	IL	114
Liberty Automotive Inc.	NY	80
Lindeco International Corp.	FL	27
LKS International	IL	35
M. S. Universal, Inc.	NJ	59
Magna Automotive Industries	NY	80
Meridian Parts Corporation	CA	10
Mondo-Comm Int'l Ltd.	NJ	60
Morris Bros. Auto Trucks & Parts Corp.	NY	82
Moss, Paul E. & Company Inc.	NY	82
Motorex Sales Corp.	NY	82
On Time Development, Inc.	NY	83
Onyx Enterprises, Inc.	NY	83
Orbis International, Ltd.	CA	12
Pac-Rim Im-Ex	WA	107
Parts Overseas Corporation	FL	27
Prior, John Inc.	NY	83
Protrade International	ME	42
Quest International	HI	31
Regalis USA, Inc.	CA	14
Rexton Corp.	FL	28

Robb, R. Int'l Associates, Inc.	MI	49	Tradex International, Inc.	CA	17
Robco International Corporation	IL	38	TWT International	OR	97
San Pedro Products, Co.	FL	28	United Export Corporation	IN	40
Schwanke Int'l Marketing Corp.	IN	40	United Exporters Service, Inc.	KY	41
Sibco, Inc.	CT	20	UTAC America Inc.	NY	88
Skyex Inc.	FL	29	VIE International Inc.	CT	20
State Export Corporation	PA	101	Whittaker, Benjamin Inc.	NY	90
Sterling International Corp.	NY	86	Wiesman & Company, Inc.	AZ	1
Taurus Shipping & Trading Co.	OH	95	Worldwide Trade Opportunities, Inc.	CA	18
Teleport Corporation	NJ	61	Zeller World Trade Corp.	OH	96
Trade Com International Inc.	OH	95	Zuniga International	FL	29
Trade Development Corp. of Chicago	CA	16			

7. BUILDING MATERIALS

A B International	CA	1	International Consolidated Exchange	OH	93
AGB International Management Corp.	NY	66	International Enterprises	TN	118
AME Matex Corp.	NJ	54	Internet Corporation USA	WA	107
Amerasia Trading Co., Inc.	CA	2	Intertrade Services, Inc.	NJ	116
American Amenities, Inc.	CA	111	Intraco Corporation	MI	48
American Export Trading Co.	CA	2	ISIS International Export Mgmt. Co.	UT	105
Amtrade International Corp.	CA	3	ITBR, Inc.	TX	104
Anaheim Marketing International	CA	3	J & M Company, Ltd.	IL	35
ARC International Group, Inc.	MA	45	Jahn, Henry R. & Son, Inc.	NY	78
Avalon Group, Ltd.	CA	4	Jajin Trading and Marketing, Inc.	WA	107
Bay World Trading, Ltd.	CA	4	JDRAS Enterprises, Inc.	NJ	58
Bogart International Sales	OH	92	Kallman Associates	NJ	117
Bryan, Errol H. International	NY	68	Kammeh Int'l Trade Co.	IL	35
Davis Elliott International Inc.	PA	98	L & W Equipment Corporation	CA	9
Domestic & International Technology	PA	98	Levinson, Samuel & Associates, Inc.	IL	114
Donovan, W. J. Co.	NY	70	Marcus and Weimer, Inc.	OH	94
Drake America	NY	71	McKim Group	MA	46
Dynacon	MO	50	Midwest Enterprises	WI	109
Eagle International Enterprises, Inc.	CA	5	Midwestern Trading Corp.	IL	36
EX-IM U.S.A., Inc.	IL	33	Natcom International	OH	94
Expomar International Inc.	NJ	56	New Mexico Int'l Trade & Devel. Co.	NM	62
Expotech	GA	30	New World Management, Inc.	NY	82
F. P. Intersales Corporation	FL	25	Nikiforov, George, Inc.	NY	83
Ferrex International, Inc.	NY	72	Oliver Resource Group, Inc.	CA	11
Fields International	IL	33	Onyx Enterprises, Inc.	NY	83
Gladex Corporation	CA	6	Overseas Services Corp.	IL	36
Global Marketing Services, Inc.	FL	25	Pac-Rim Im-Ex	WA	107
Global Merchandising Corp.	CA	6	Piedmont Caribbean Trade Limited	NC	52
Glynn International, Inc.	MA	46	Prestige U.S. Exports	FL	27
Grable, John Exports, Inc.	FL	25	Products Corp. of North America, Inc.	OR	97
Grand Pacific Finance Corp.	NY	74	Protrade International	ME	42
Hall & Reis, Inc.	NY	76	Quatro International, Inc.	FL	28
Hemisol Export & Import Corp.	FL	26	Rajiv International, Inc.	MD	44
Heritage International Inc.	CA	7	Rivard International Corp.	OH	95
IFRAS, Inc.	NY	77	Robco International Corporation	IL	38
Inter Euro Trading, Inc.	NY	78	Roldan Products Corporation	MO	50

Saria International, Inc.	CA	15	United Gulf Services, Inc.	CA	17
Saris Corp.	WA	108	UTAC America Inc.	NY	88
Sharoubim International Group, Inc.	NY	84	Verde America, Inc.	NY	90
Trade Com International Inc.	OH	95	Wiesman & Company, Inc.	AZ	1
Tradex International/Div. of United	OH	96	Wolfson, P. J. Co., Inc.	NY	91
Trans Tech Management Consulting	IL	115	World-Trade Services, Inc.	OH	96
Turnkey Projects, Inc.	OR	118	XPORT, Port Authority Trading Co.	NY	91
United Exporters Service, Inc.	KY	41	Yagi, S. Inc., dba Primex, Inc.	CA	18

8. CHEMICALS, CHEMICAL & PETROCHEMICAL INDUSTRIES EQUIPMENT & PRODUCTS

Abaco International Corp.	CA	2	Hemisol Export & Import Corp.	FL	26
Acarex, Inc.	NY	64	High Technology Export Services, Inc.	DC	113
Akron Overseas Inc.	OH	92	Import Export Management Svc., Inc.	TX	104
All American Commodities, Inc.	FL	21	INSECO, Inc.	NY	77
Allied Systems Export Corp.	PA	97	International Consolidated Exchange	OH	93
Amerasia Trading Co., Inc.	CA	2	International Controls Co., Inc.	PA	100
AmTrade Aid, Inc.	NJ	116	International ICS Group Inc.	CA	111
Amtrade International Corp.	CA	3	International Industries Corp.	SC	102
ARC International Group, Inc.	MA	45	International Product Mktg. Group Inc.	CA	9
Asia Marketing & Consulting Corp.	UT	105	International Purchasers	MD	43
Atlas Asia-Pacific	CA	3	International Trades	CA	111
Berkowitz, N. C. & Company	CA	4	Intertrade Services, Inc.	NJ	116
Boar's Head Int'l Trading Co.	WA	106	ITBR, Inc.	TX	104
Bock Pharmaceutical, Inc.	OH	92	J & M Company, Ltd.	IL	35
British-American Forfaiting Co., Inc.	MO	116	Kalamazoo International, Inc.	MI	48
Caravan Export Corp.	NY	68	Kammeh Int'l Trade Co.	IL	35
Chazen Industrial Corp.	NJ	55	Kip Company, The	OH	118
Chemical Export Company, Inc.	MA	45	Levinson, Samuel & Associates, Inc.	IL	114
Chicago Import/Export Consultants	IL	114	Lotus Group, The	NC	52
Curtis TradeGroup, Inc.	IN	38	M. S. Universal, Inc.	NJ	59
Debco Chemicals Sales, Co.	NY	70	McKim Group	MA	46
Domestic & International Technology	PA	98	Midwest Enterprises	WI	109
Dunlap Export Co., Inc.	OH	92	Minthorne Int'l Company	NY	81
Dunlap International	IA	40	Moss, Paul E. & Company Inc.	NY	82
Eagle International Enterprises, Inc.	CA	5	Muni Trading Co., Inc.	NJ	60
Electrical Manufacturers Export Co.	ME	42	New World Management, Inc.	NY	82
Exmart International, Inc.	NJ	56	Nikiforov, George, Inc.	NY	83
Expomar International Inc.	NJ	56	Onyx Enterprises, Inc.	NY	83
Export Consultant Service	PA	98	Orion International & Company, Inc.	CO	19
F. P. Intersales Corporation	FL	25	Pan Pacific International	CA	13
Fame International	TX	103	Pegasus International Corp.	NJ	60
FMI Automotive Corp./FMI Trading	NY	73	PNR International, Ltd.	IL	37
Global Dimensions Corp.	TX	118	Prestige U.S. Exports	FL	27
Globelink Incorporated	TX	104	Raba Corporation	HI	114
Glynn International, Inc.	MA	46	RKF International Inc.	IL	37
Grand Pacific Finance Corp.	NY	74	Robco International Corporation	IL	38
Hall & Reis, Inc.	NY	76	Rodriguez, R.A., Inc.	NY	84
Hardy, M. W. & Co, Inc.	NY	76	Sacks, Harvey C. Export Consulting	CA	15
HCI Corporation	VA	106	Semsco International	FL	28

Sharoubim International Group, Inc.	NY	84		VIE International Inc.	CT	20
Strato Enterprises	NJ	61		Wellesley International Corp.	MA	47
Technic Group	TN	103		Witz Scientific, Inc.	OH	96
Tecnomaster Int'l Corp.	NJ	61		World-Trade Services, Inc.	OH	96
Timcorp Int'l Marketing Co., Ltd.	HI	31		Worldwide Trade Opportunities, Inc.	CA	18
Trade Com International Inc.	OH	95		XPORT, Port Authority Trading Co.	NY	91
Tradex International, Inc.	CA	17		Yagi, S. Inc., dba Primex, Inc.	CA	18
Tradex International/Div. of United	OH	96		Zuniga International	FL	29
Tratech International, Inc.	AL	111				

9. COMMUNICATION EQUIPMENT & SYSTEMS

A & S International Marketing Co., Inc.	NY	64		Intrax	MA	46
Abaco International Corp.	CA	2		ITBR, Inc.	TX	104
Actrade International Corp.	NY	64		Items Unlimited	NJ	116
Alkier Consulting (Consult U.S.A., Inc.)	IL	114		ITM Corporation	CA	112
Amerasia Trading Co., Inc.	CA	2		IVEX International	NH	53
American Eagle Purchasing Agents	MA	44		Kallman Associates	NJ	117
Amex, Inc.	MN	49		Levinson, Samuel & Associates, Inc.	IL	114
AmTrade Aid, Inc.	NJ	116		M International Export (MINTEX)	VA	106
ARC International Group, Inc.	MA	45		Marketshare Inc.	MA	115
Atlantech Inc.	FL	22		Mercatus International, Inc.	CA	10
Berkowitz, N. C. & Company	CA	4		Minthorne Int'l Company	NY	81
Caravan Export Corp.	NY	68		MK Technology/Deltac	DC	113
Cobble Hill International	MA	45		Natcom International	OH	94
Consultants International, Ltd.	CT	112		Nesa Corporation	CT	20
Dage Corporation	CT	19		New Mexico Int'l Trade & Devel. Co.	NM	62
Daretel Group, Inc., The	IL	32		Ohio Overseas Corporation	OH	94
Dibma Enterprises, Inc.	FL	24		Orbis International, Ltd.	CA	12
EMB Trading Co.	NY	72		Pacific Export Services, Inc.	TX	105
Expo International Co., Inc.	NJ	56		Proxima Inc.	NY	84
G.D.E., Inc.	CA	5		Quatro International, Inc.	FL	28
Gas International Corp., The	NJ	57		Reed, Charles H. Export, Inc.	MA	46
Global Technology, Inc.	CA	6		Regalis USA, Inc.	CA	14
Globelink Incorporated	TX	104		RHA Group	CA	14
Glynn International, Inc.	MA	46		Roburn Agencies Inc.	NY	84
Grand Pacific Finance Corp.	NY	74		Row International, Inc.	CA	15
Haller, Mart Inc.	FL	26		Sacks, Harvey C. Export Consulting	CA	15
Hemisol Export & Import Corp.	FL	26		Sharoubim International Group, Inc.	NY	84
High Technology Export Services, Inc.	DC	113		Silicon International	CA	16
IMEX Trading, Ltd.	CA	8		Skyex Inc.	FL	29
Imtrex Corporation	OH	93		Smythe International Services	CA	112
INEX International	CA	8		Spivey, James S., Inc.	MD	44
INEX Technology International	MD	43		Strato Enterprises	NJ	61
International Communications, Inc.	MA	115		Sylvan Ginsbury Ltd.	NJ	61
International Computer Systems	CA	9		Symbicon Associates, Inc.	NH	53
International Information Specialists	CA	111		Technic Group	TN	103
International Marketing Services Co.	WA	107		Trade Development Corp. of Chicago	CA	16
Intertrade Services, Inc.	NJ	116		Universal Data Consultants, Inc.	GA	31
Intra-World Export Co., Inc.	NY	78		Wellesley International Corp.	MA	47

| Wiesman & Company, Inc. | AZ | 1 |
| World-Trade Services, Inc. | OH | 96 |

| Worldwide Exporters, Inc. | CA | 18 |
| XPORT, Port Authority Trading Co. | NY | 91 |

10. COMPUTERS, PERIPHERALS, BUSINESS EQUIPMENT & SOFTWARE

313 R/E Ltd.	NY	64	ITM Corporation	CA	112
Abaco International Corp.	CA	2	IVEX International	NH	53
Actrade International Corp.	NY	64	Kallman Associates	NJ	117
Alkier Consulting (Consult U.S.A., Inc.)	IL	114	Kammeh Int'l Trade Co.	IL	35
Amerasia Trading Co., Inc.	CA	2	Levinson, Samuel & Associates, Inc.	IL	114
Amex, Inc.	MN	49	Mancor	WA	119
AmTech Organization Inc.	MA	44	Marketshare Inc.	MA	115
AmTrade Aid, Inc.	NJ	116	Mercatus International, Inc.	CA	10
Amtrade International Corp.	CA	3	Micro Informatica Corp.	FL	27
ARC International Group, Inc.	MA	45	MK Technology/Deltac	DC	113
Atlantech Inc.	FL	22	Natcom International	OH	94
Automotive International Corp.	TX	103	New Mexico Int'l Trade & Devel. Co.	NM	62
Bay World Trading, Ltd.	CA	4	New World Management, Inc.	NY	82
Beijing Trade Exchange, Inc.	DC	21	Orbis International, Ltd.	CA	12
Berkowitz, N. C. & Company	CA	4	Pacific Export Services, Inc.	TX	105
Boar's Head Int'l Trading Co.	WA	106	PNR International, Ltd.	IL	37
Caravan Export Corp.	NY	68	Prestige U.S. Exports	FL	27
Chihade International, Inc.	GA	29	Proxima Inc.	NY	84
Cobble Hill International	MA	45	RHA Group	CA	14
Computer Commodities Int'l	MN	49	Roldan Products Corporation	MO	50
CPS Marketing Corp.	FL	23	Row International, Inc.	CA	15
Dibma Enterprises, Inc.	FL	24	Sacks, Harvey C. Export Consulting	CA	15
Ewig, Carl F. Inc.	NJ	56	Sharoubim International Group, Inc.	NY	84
Expotech	GA	30	Silicon International	CA	16
Fame International	TX	103	Skyex Inc.	FL	29
Fernandez Import/Export, Inc. USA	NC	50	Smythe International Services	CA	112
G.D.E., Inc.	CA	5	Software Export Corp.	MA	47
General Product Co., Inc.	NJ	57	Strato Enterprises	NJ	61
Global Technology, Inc.	CA	6	Surel International, Inc.	MA	47
Glynn International, Inc.	MA	46	Sylvan Ginsbury Ltd.	NJ	61
Grand Pacific Finance Corp.	NY	74	Symbicon Associates, Inc.	NH	53
Hallmarkets International, Ltd.	NY	76	TechBridge Marketing	GA	30
High Technology Export Services, Inc.	DC	113	Third Party International	OR	97
IMEX Trading, Ltd.	CA	8	Trade Development Corp. of Chicago	CA	16
Import Export Management Svc., Inc.	TX	104	Tradelink, Inc.	ID	31
INEX International	CA	8	Tradex International, Inc.	CA	17
INEX Technology International	MD	43	Tradex International	OH	96
Interconsult	NH	116	United Exporters Co.	CA	17
International Business Resources Inc.	HI	114	Universal Data Consultants, Inc.	GA	31
International Communications, Inc.	MA	115	Vanguard Int'l Management Services	NY	90
International Computer Systems	CA	9	Vensamar Export Management	AL	1
International Controls Co., Inc.	PA	100	VIE International Inc.	CT	20
International Information Specialists	CA	111	Wolfson, P. J. Co., Inc.	NY	91
International Marketing Services Co.	WA	107	Worldwide Exporters, Inc.	CA	18
Intertrade Services, Inc.	NJ	116	Worldwide Trade Opportunities, Inc.	CA	18
ISIS International Export Mgmt. Co.	UT	105	XPORT, Port Authority Trading Co.	NY	91

11. CONSTRUCTION EQUIPMENT

A B International	CA	1	Hemisol Export & Import Corp.	FL	26
Abaco International Corp.	CA	2	Heritage International Inc.	CA	7
Acarex, Inc.	NY	64	Hoffman International, Inc.	NJ	58
Actrade International Corp.	NY	64	International Consolidated Exchange	OH	93
AGB International Management Corp.	NY	66	International Information Specialists	CA	111
Amerasia Trading Co., Inc.	CA	2	International Marketing Consultants	IL	34
American Export Trading Co.	CA	2	International Purchasers	MD	43
Amex, Inc.	MN	49	Intertrade Services, Inc.	NJ	116
AmTrade Aid, Inc.	NJ	116	ITM Corporation	CA	112
Amtrade International Corp.	CA	3	J & M Sales Corporation	NJ	58
ARC International Group, Inc.	MA	45	Levinson, Samuel & Associates, Inc.	IL	114
Asia Marketing & Consulting Corp.	UT	105	Lotus Group, The	NC	52
Automotive International Corp.	TX	103	McKim Group	MA	46
Avalon Group, Ltd.	CA	4	McLean International Marketing, Inc.	WI	108
Browne International Industries, Inc.	NY	68	Midwestern Trading Corp.	IL	36
Caravan Export Corp.	NY	68	New Mexico Int'l Trade & Devel. Co.	NM	62
Chaco International, Inc.	CA	5	Orbis International, Ltd.	CA	12
Charon-Jessam Trading Co. Inc.	NY	69	Pacific Export Services, Inc.	TX	105
Domestic & International Technology	PA	98	Protrade International	ME	42
Donovan, W. J. Co.	NY	70	Provident Traders, Inc.	CA	13
Eagle International Enterprises, Inc.	CA	5	Quatro International, Inc.	FL	28
Engineering Equipment Co.	IL	33	Rivard International Corp.	OH	95
Expomar International Inc.	NJ	56	Rocky Mountain Export Co., Inc.	CO	19
Fields International	IL	33	Sharoubim International Group, Inc.	NY	84
FWD International, Inc.	IL	34	Technic Group	TN	103
Geonex International Corp.	NY	74	Tecnomaster Int'l Corp.	NJ	61
Gladex Corporation	CA	6	Trade Development Corp. of Chicago	CA	16
Glynn International, Inc.	MA	46	Tradex International	OH	96
Gomez, Manuel and Associates, Inc.	FL	25	United Gulf Services, Inc.	CA	17
Grable, John Exports, Inc.	FL	25	Verde America, Inc.	NY	90
Hall & Reis, Inc.	NY	76	World-Trade Services, Inc.	OH	96

12. CONSUMER SERVICE INDUSTRIES: SPECIALIZED MACHINERY & EQUIPMENT

Allied Systems Export Corp.	PA	97	Expotech	GA	30
American Amenities, Inc.	CA	111	Fremont Group Limited	IL	114
American Export Trading Co.	CA	2	Geonex International Corp.	NY	74
AmTrade Aid, Inc.	NJ	116	Global Technology, Inc.	CA	6
Aztek International Corp.	IN	38	Globelink Incorporated	TX	104
Ballagh & Thrall, Inc.	PA	98	Glynn International, Inc.	MA	46
Boar's Head Int'l Trading Co.	WA	106	Hall & Reis, Inc.	NY	76
British-American Forfaiting Co., Inc.	MO	116	Hosler & Associates, Inc.	MO	50
Caravan Export Corp.	NY	68	International Information Specialists	CA	111
Davidson International	NJ	55	ISIS International Export Mgmt. Co.	UT	105
Domestic & International Technology	PA	98	Kammeh Int'l Trade Co.	IL	35
Donovan, W. J. Co.	NY	70	Levinson, Samuel & Associates, Inc.	IL	114
Ewig, Carl F. Inc.	NJ	56	MK Technology/Deltac	DC	113
EX-IM U.S.A., Inc.	IL	33	Mondo-Comm Int'l Ltd.	NJ	60

Nikiforov, George, Inc.	NY	83
Pegasus International Corp.	NJ	60
Quest International	HI	31
Silo International, Inc.	NY	86
Smythe International Services	CA	112

Trade Com International Inc.	OH	95
Turnkey Projects, Inc.	OR	118
Wiesman & Company, Inc.	AZ	1
Wolfson, P. J. Co., Inc.	NY	91
ZED Group, Inc.	MA	47

13. ELECTRICAL, RADIO & TELEVISION, EQUIPMENT AND PARTS

Abaco International Corp.	CA	2
American Export Trading Co.	CA	2
AmTrade Aid, Inc.	NJ	116
ARC International Group, Inc.	MA	45
Asch Trading Co.	NY	67
Asia Marketing & Consulting Corp.	UT	105
Ballagh & Thrall, Inc.	PA	98
Beijing Trade Exchange, Inc.	DC	21
Berns, M., Industries, Inc.	NY	67
Cobble Hill International	MA	45
Curtis TradeGroup, Inc.	IN	38
Dage Corporation	CT	19
Davidson International	NJ	55
Dibma Enterprises, Inc.	FL	24
Drake America	NY	71
Electrical Manufacturers Export Co.	ME	42
Electrical Sales Corp. Int'l	FL	24
EMB Trading Co.	NY	72
Expo International Co., Inc.	NJ	56
F. P. Intersales Corporation	FL	25
Fortune Enterprises International Co.	PA	100
General Product Co., Inc.	NJ	57
Global Technology, Inc.	CA	6
Haller, Mart Inc.	FL	26
Hemisol Export & Import Corp.	FL	26
High Technology Export Services, Inc.	DC	113
Holmes, Cecil Int'l Corp.	CA	7
IBEX Technical Corp.	PA	100
IMEX Trading, Ltd.	CA	8
Inter Euro Trading, Inc.	NY	78
International Consolidated Exchange	OH	93
International ICS Group Inc.	CA	111
International Information Specialists	CA	111
International Marketing Services Co.	WA	107

Intertrade Services, Inc.	NJ	116
ITBR, Inc.	TX	104
ITM Corporation	CA	112
IVEX International	NH	53
Kato International, Inc.	NJ	58
L & W Equipment Corporation	CA	9
M. S. Universal, Inc.	NJ	59
Manhattan Nassau Corp.	NY	80
Marketshare Inc.	MA	115
McKim Group	MA	46
Midwestern Trading Corp.	IL	36
Minthorne Int'l Company	NY	81
Motorex Sales Corp.	NY	82
Nesa Corporation	CT	20
Onyx Enterprises, Inc.	NY	83
Prestige U.S. Exports	FL	27
Prior, John Inc.	NY	83
Quest International	HI	31
Raba Corporation	HI	114
RHA Group	CA	14
Roburn Agencies Inc.	NY	84
Row International, Inc.	CA	15
Silicon International	CA	16
Skyex Inc.	FL	29
Surel International, Inc.	MA	47
Sylvan Ginsbury Ltd.	NJ	61
Torning International, Inc.	CT	20
Trade Development Corp. of Chicago	CA	16
Tradelink, Inc.	ID	31
Tradeways, Ltd.	VA	106
Trans International Group Ltd.	PA	102
United Exporters Service, Inc.	KY	41
Wellesley International Corp.	MA	47
World-Trade Services, Inc.	OH	96

14. FARM EQUIPMENT & PRODUCTS

A & S International Marketing Co., Inc.	NY	64
Actrade International Corp.	NY	64
AEON International Corp.	IA	40
Alkier Consulting (Consult U.S.A., Inc.)	IL	114
All American Commodities, Inc.	FL	21

American Export Trading Co.	CA	2
Amtrade International Corp.	CA	3
ARC International Group, Inc.	MA	45
Automotive International Corp.	TX	103
Aztek International Corp.	IN	38

Bio-Livestock Int'l, Inc.	NY	67	Jireh International	PA	101
Bisho, J. R. Co., Inc.	CA	4	Kalamazoo International, Inc.	MI	48
Caravan Export Corp.	NY	68	Mancor	WA	119
Chicago Midwest Export Marketing	IL	32	McKim Group	MA	46
Debco Chemicals Sales, Co.	NY	70	McLean International Marketing, Inc.	WI	108
Dunlap International	IA	40	Medica International, Ltd.	IL	36
Dynacon	MO	50	Mercator Corporation	PA	101
Eagle International Enterprises, Inc.	CA	5	Midwest Agricultural Export Corp.	WI	108
Expotech	GA	30	Morse Agri-Energy Associates	CA	112
Ferrex International, Inc.	NY	72	Neslo International Ltd.	IL	36
Fremont Group Limited	IL	114	Onyx Enterprises, Inc.	NY	83
Geonex International Corp.	NY	74	Orbis International, Ltd.	CA	12
Gladex Corporation	CA	6	Pacific Exports	CA	13
Global Dimensions Corp.	TX	118	Products Corp. of North America, Inc.	OR	97
Gomez, Manuel and Associates, Inc.	FL	25	Raba Corporation	HI	114
Hall & Reis, Inc.	NY	76	Robco International Corporation	IL	38
HCI Corporation	VA	106	Roldan Products Corporation	MO	50
Hemisol Export & Import Corp.	FL	26	San Pedro Products, Co.	FL	28
Hockman Lewis Limited	NJ	57	Saris Corp.	WA	108
International Consolidated Exchange	OH	93	Technic Group	TN	103
International Marketing Consultants	IL	34	Trade Development Corp. of Chicago	CA	16
International Marketing Systems, Ltd.	ND	52	Tradex International, Inc.	CA	17
Iowa Export Import Trading Co.	IA	41	United Exporters Service, Inc.	KY	41
ITM Corporation	CA	112	Wiesman & Company, Inc.	AZ	1
J & M Sales Corporation	NJ	58	World-Trade Services, Inc.	OH	96
Jahn, Henry R. & Son, Inc.	NY	78	Yagi, S. Inc., dba Primex, Inc.	CA	18

15. FOOD PROCESSING/PACKAGING MACHINERY & EQUIPMENT

A & S International Marketing Co., Inc.	NY	64	Eagle International Enterprises, Inc.	CA	5
Ad. Auriema Inc.	NY	66	EX-IM U.S.A., Inc.	IL	33
Allied Systems Export Corp.	PA	97	Exmart International, Inc.	NJ	56
AME Matex Corp.	NJ	54	Expomar International Inc.	NJ	56
American Enterprise Co.	CA	2	Expotech	GA	30
AmTrade Aid, Inc.	NJ	116	F. P. Intersales Corporation	FL	25
Anaheim Marketing International	CA	3	Fame International	TX	103
Asia Marketing & Consulting Corp.	UT	105	Fleetwood International	NY	73
Aztek International Corp.	IN	38	Gas International Corp., The	NJ	57
BMIL International	NY	67	Geonex International Corp.	NY	74
Boar's Head Int'l Trading Co.	WA	106	Glynn International, Inc.	MA	46
Borco Engineering Co.	WI	108	IFRAS, Inc.	NY	77
Bryan, Errol H. International	NY	68	Inter-America Sales Co., Inc.	LA	42
Chew International	NY	69	International Projects, Inc.	OH	93
Chicago Import/Export Consultants	IL	114	ISIS International Export Mgmt. Co.	UT	105
Chicago Midwest Export Marketing	IL	32	ITBR, Inc.	TX	104
Chihade International, Inc.	GA	29	Jitch, Harry & Sons	NY	78
Cobo, J. & Associates, Inc.	FL	23	Kalglas International Inc.	NY	79
Domestic & International Technology	PA	98	Klockner Ina Industrial Installations	NY	79
Donovan, W. J. Co.	NY	70	Lanla Sales	NY	80
Dorian America	NY	70	Mancor	WA	119
Dunlap International	IA	40	McLean International Marketing, Inc.	WI	108

16. FOOD PRODUCTS & BEVERAGES

17. FURNITURE

AEON International Corp.	IA	40	Intertrade, Inc.	MI	48
Alkier Consulting (Consult U.S.A., Inc.)	IL	114	J & M Company, Ltd.	IL	35
Amas International, Inc.	FL	22	Kammeh Int'l Trade Co.	IL	35
American Amenities, Inc.	CA	111	Lotus Group, The	NC	52
American Trade International Corp.	UT	105	M & P Export Management Corp.	NJ	59
Asia Marketing & Consulting Corp.	UT	105	McLean International Marketing, Inc.	WI	108
Avalon Group, Ltd.	CA	4	Midwestern Trading Corp.	IL	36
CPS Marketing Corp.	FL	23	New Mexico Int'l Trade & Devel. Co.	NM	62
Davidson International	NJ	55	Ohio Overseas Corporation	OH	94
Fernandez Import/Export, Inc. USA	NC	50	Pacific Export Services, Inc.	TX	105
Global Marketing Concepts	NC	52	Products Corp. of North America, Inc.	OR	97
Globelink Incorporated	TX	104	Protrade International	ME	42
Import Export Management Svc., Inc.	TX	104	Roldan Products Corporation	MO	50
Inter Euro Trading, Inc.	NY	78	Romac Export Management Corp.	CA	14
International Projects, Inc.	OH	93	United Gulf Services, Inc.	CA	17
International Trades	CA	111	Verde America, Inc.	NY	90
Internet Corporation USA	WA	107	XPORT, Port Authority Trading Co.	NY	91

18. GAMES, TOYS, ETC.

Abaco International Corp.	CA	2	Jitch, Harry & Sons	NY	78
Actrade International Corp.	NY	64	Kalglas International Inc.	NY	79
Alkier Consulting (Consult U.S.A., Inc.)	IL	114	Kraemer Mercantile Corp.	NY	79
Aztek International Corp.	IN	38	M & P Export Management Corp.	NJ	59
C. International	NJ	54	Mirage Products International, Inc.	CA	11
Celestial Mercantile Corp.	NY	68	Natcom International	OH	94
CPS Marketing Corp.	FL	23	Nelson, Edward International, Inc.	CA	11
Davidson International	NJ	55	Pacific Export Services, Inc.	TX	105
Frontier Trading	CA	111	Quest International	HI	31
General Product Co., Inc.	NJ	57	Regalis USA, Inc.	CA	14
Global Merchandising Corp.	CA	6	RKF International Inc.	IL	37
Globelink Incorporated	TX	104	Romac Export Management Corp.	CA	14
IFRAS, Inc.	NY	77	Smythe International Services	CA	112
Import Export Management Svc., Inc.	TX	104	Strong Trading Company	NH	53
Intercontinental Enterprises Ltd.	CA	9	TRADECO Association of N.Y., Ltd.	NY	87
International ICS Group Inc.	CA	111	Universial Export Agencies	NY	88
Intra-World Export Co., Inc.	NY	78	Viking Traders Inc.	NJ	62
ITM Corporation	CA	112			

19. GASOLINES, LUBRICANTS & EQUIPMENT

A & S International Marketing Co., Inc.	NY	64	Celestial Mercantile Corp.	NY	68
Actrade International Corp.	NY	64	Chicago Import/Export Consultants	IL	114
Amas International, Inc.	FL	22	Davis Elliott International Inc.	PA	98
Avalon Group, Ltd.	CA	4	Domestic & International Technology	PA	98
British-American Forfaiting Co., Inc.	MO	116	Dreyco, Inc.	NJ	55

Eagle International Enterprises, Inc.	CA	5	Nikiforov, George, Inc.	NY	83
Expotech	GA	30	Ohio Overseas Corporation	OH	94
Geonex International Corp.	NY	74	Overseas Operations Inc.	CA	12
Gomez, Manuel and Associates, Inc.	FL	25	Prior, John Inc.	NY	83
Hockman Lewis Limited	NJ	57	San Pedro Products, Co.	FL	28
International Enterprises	TN	118	Saria International, Inc.	CA	15
International Product Mktg. Group Inc.	CA	9	Silo International, Inc.	NY	86
International Trades	CA	111	TRADECO Association of N.Y., Ltd.	NY	87
Intertrade Services, Inc.	NJ	116	Tradex International, Inc.	CA	17
Karl, Peter A., International Sales	NY	79	United Gulf Services, Inc.	CA	17
Moss, Paul E. & Company Inc.	NY	82	Zuniga International	FL	29

20. GRAPHIC ARTS, PRINTING EQUIPMENT & SUPPLIES

Amas International, Inc.	FL	22	Lotus Group, The	NC	52
ARC International Group, Inc.	MA	45	Matthews Globus Trading, Ltd.	PA	101
Atali-Mare, Ltd.	GA	29	Natcom International	OH	94
Ballagh & Thrall, Inc.	PA	98	Nelson, Edward International, Inc.	CA	11
C. International	NJ	54	Proxima Inc.	NY	84
Davis Elliott International Inc.	PA	98	RKF International Inc.	IL	37
Debco Chemicals Sales, Co.	NY	70	Roldan Products Corporation	MO	50
Dreyco, Inc.	NJ	55	Romac Export Management Corp.	CA	14
ERW International Inc.	IL	33	Row International, Inc.	CA	15
Gate Group U.S.A., Inc.	NY	73	Trans Tech Management Consulting	IL	115
Gladex Corporation	CA	6	Universal Data Consultants, Inc.	GA	31
Import Export Management Svc., Inc.	TX	104	Wolfson, P. J. Co., Inc.	NY	91
International Trades	CA	111	Worldwide Exporters, Inc.	CA	18
Levinson, Samuel & Associates, Inc.	IL	114			

21. HARDWARE

Actrade International Corp.	NY	64	F. P. Intersales Corporation	FL	25
Amas International, Inc.	FL	22	Fields International	IL	33
AME Matex Corp.	NJ	54	Geonex International Corp.	NY	74
American Amenities, Inc.	CA	111	Globelink Incorporated	TX	104
Amtrade International Corp.	CA	3	Grable, John Exports, Inc.	FL	25
ARC International Group, Inc.	MA	45	Grand Pacific Finance Corp.	NY	74
Avalon Group, Ltd.	CA	4	Hall & Reis, Inc.	NY	76
Aztek International Corp.	IN	38	Hallmarkets International, Ltd.	NY	76
Bogart International Sales	OH	92	Hemisol Export & Import Corp.	FL	26
C. International	NJ	54	Hyman, Harry & Son, Inc.	NY	76
Celestial Mercantile Corp.	NY	68	International Communications, Inc.	MA	115
Chew International	NY	69	International Marketing Consultants	IL	34
Dage Corporation	CT	19	International Product Mktg. Group Inc.	CA	9
Drake America	NY	71	International Trades	CA	111
Dreyco, Inc.	NJ	55	Intra-World Export Co., Inc.	NY	78
Dreyfus & Associates, Ltd.	NY	71	J & M Company, Ltd.	IL	35
Export Trade of America, Inc.	NY	72	Kalglas International Inc.	NY	79
Expotech	GA	30	Karl, Peter A., International Sales	NY	79

Latco International, Inc.	SC	102	San Pedro Products, Co.	FL	28
Lotus Group, The	NC	52	Saria International, Inc.	CA	15
M & P Export Management Corp.	NJ	59	Semsco International	FL	28
Marcus and Weimer, Inc.	OH	94	Silo International, Inc.	NY	86
McKim Group	MA	46	Smythe International Services	CA	112
Nikiforov, George, Inc.	NY	83	Trade Com International Inc.	OH	95
Overseas Operations Inc.	CA	12	Trans Tech Management Consulting	IL	115
Protrade International	ME	42	United Export Corporation	IN	40
Proxima Inc.	NY	84	United Gulf Services, Inc.	CA	17
Regalis USA, Inc.	CA	14	Universal Data Consultants, Inc.	GA	31
Rivard International Corp.	OH	95	Vensamar Export Management	AL	1
RKF International Inc.	IL	37	ZED Group, Inc.	MA	47
Romac Export Management Corp.	CA	14			

22. HEATING, AIR-CONDITIONING AND REFRIGERATION

Actrade International Corp.	NY	64	L & W Equipment Corporation	CA	9
Ad. Auriema Inc.	NY	66	M. S. Universal, Inc.	NJ	59
AGB International Management Corp.	NY	66	Manhattan Nassau Corp.	NY	80
Alkier Consulting (Consult U.S.A., Inc.)	IL	114	Marcus and Weimer, Inc.	OH	94
Amas International, Inc.	FL	22	Medica International, Ltd.	IL	36
AME Matex Corp.	NJ	54	Mercator Corporation	PA	101
American Amenities, Inc.	CA	111	Nagro-Berry International	IN	39
Amex, Inc.	MN	49	Natcom International	OH	94
AmTrade Aid, Inc.	NJ	116	Nikiforov, George, Inc.	NY	83
Bauer, Alex & Co.	NJ	54	Onyx Enterprises, Inc.	NY	83
BMIL International	NY	67	Orbis International, Ltd.	CA	12
Caravan Export Corp.	NY	68	Orion International & Company, Inc.	CO	19
Continental Enterprises	CA	5	Overseas Operations Inc.	CA	12
Domestic & International Technology	PA	98	PNR International, Ltd.	IL	37
Eagle International Enterprises, Inc.	CA	5	Prestige U.S. Exports	FL	27
Electrical Sales Corp. Int'l	FL	24	Rebel, Albert & Associates, Inc.	CA	14
Euroscand, Inc.	FL	24	RKF International Inc.	IL	37
Fleetwood International	NY	73	Robco International Corporation	IL	38
Gas International Corp., The	NJ	57	San Pedro Products, Co.	FL	28
Geonex International Corp.	NY	74	Saria International, Inc.	CA	15
Global Merchandising Corp.	CA	6	Sheldon, H.D. & Company, Inc.	NY	86
Hall & Reis, Inc.	NY	76	Silo International, Inc.	NY	86
Haller, Mart Inc.	FL	26	Tecnomaster Int'l Corp.	NJ	61
Hemisol Export & Import Corp.	FL	26	Tradex International	OH	96
Holmes, Cecil Int'l Corp.	CA	7	Tradex International, Inc.	CA	17
Inter-America Sales Co., Inc.	LA	42	United Export Corporation	IN	40
International Consolidated Exchange	OH	93	United Exporters Service, Inc.	KY	41
International Marketing Consultants	IL	34	USExport, Inc.	NY	88
International Projects, Inc.	OH	93	UTAC America Inc.	NY	88
Intraco Corporation	MI	48	Wiesman & Company, Inc.	AZ	1
Kallman Associates	NJ	117	Wolfson, P. J. Co., Inc.	NY	91
Kewanee International, Inc.	NJ	59	Worldwide Exporters, Inc.	CA	18

23. HOUSEHOLD FURNISHINGS & APPLIANCES

Abaco International Corp.	CA	2	Intra-World Export Co., Inc.	NY	78
Amas International, Inc.	FL	22	ISIS International Export Mgmt. Co.	UT	105
American Amenities, Inc.	CA	111	J & M Company, Ltd.	IL	35
American Trade International Corp.	UT	105	Kraemer Mercantile Corp.	NY	79
Amtrade International Corp.	CA	3	M. S. Universal, Inc.	NJ	59
Anaheim Marketing International	CA	3	Manhattan Nassau Corp.	NY	80
Aztek International Corp.	IN	38	Midwestern Trading Corp.	IL	36
C. International	NJ	54	Onyx Enterprises, Inc.	NY	83
Chihade International, Inc.	GA	29	Overseas Operations Inc.	CA	12
Comtrade International Inc.	NY	70	Pacific Export Services, Inc.	TX	105
Davidson International	NJ	55	Prior, John Inc.	NY	83
Dunlap Export Co., Inc.	OH	92	Protrade International	ME	42
Ewig, Carl F. Inc.	NJ	56	Quatro International, Inc.	FL	28
Exmart International, Inc.	NJ	56	Regalis USA, Inc.	CA	14
Export Trade of America, Inc.	NY	72	RKF International Inc.	IL	37
General Product Co., Inc.	NJ	57	Roldan Products Corporation	MO	50
Gerber, J. & Co., Inc.	NY	74	Romac Export Management Corp.	CA	14
Globelink Incorporated	TX	104	Sheldon, H.D. & Company, Inc.	NY	86
Hemisol Export & Import Corp.	FL	26	Silo International, Inc.	NY	86
Hyman, Harry & Son, Inc.	NY	76	UTAC America Inc.	NY	88
International ICS Group Inc.	CA	111	Wellesley International Corp.	MA	47
International Marketing Consultants	IL	34	XPORT, Port Authority Trading Co.	NY	91
Intertrade, Inc.	MI	48			

24. INDUSTRIAL PRODUCTS & EQUIPMENT

A & S International Marketing Co., Inc.	NY	64	Curtis TradeGroup, Inc.	IN	38
Actrade International Corp.	NY	64	Dage Corporation	CT	19
Ad. Auriema Inc.	NY	66	Davis Elliott International Inc.	PA	98
AGB International Management Corp.	NY	66	Debco Chemicals Sales, Co.	NY	70
Allied Systems Export Corp.	PA	97	Domestic & International Technology	PA	98
Amas International, Inc.	FL	22	Drake America	NY	71
Amerasia Trading Co., Inc.	CA	2	Dreyco, Inc.	NJ	55
Amex, Inc.	MN	49	Dynacon	MO	50
AmTrade Aid, Inc.	NJ	116	E & G International, Inc.	FL	24
Amtrade International Corp.	CA	3	Eagle International Enterprises, Inc.	CA	5
ARC International Group, Inc.	MA	45	EMB Trading Co.	NY	72
Automotive Export Inc.	FL	22	Engineering Equipment Co.	IL	33
Avalon Group, Ltd.	CA	4	EX-IM U.S.A., Inc.	IL	33
Aztek International Corp.	IN	38	Export Consultant Service	PA	98
Bauer, Alex & Co.	NJ	54	Export Procedures Co.	PA	99
Bogart International Sales	OH	92	Far East Trade & Investment Co.	PA	99
Borco Engineering Co.	WI	108	Fields International	IL	33
British-American Forfaiting Co., Inc.	MO	116	FMI Automotive Corp./FMI Trading	NY	73
Browne International Industries, Inc.	NY	68	Fortune Enterprises International Co.	PA	100
Caravan Export Corp.	NY	68	Geonex International Corp.	NY	74
Chemical Export Company, Inc.	MA	45	Gladex Corporation	CA	6
Chicago Import/Export Consultants	IL	114	Glynn International, Inc.	MA	46

Grand Pacific Finance Corp.	NY	74	Rebel, Albert & Associates, Inc.	CA	14
Hall & Reis, Inc.	NY	76	Rivard International Corp.	OH	95
High Technology Export Services, Inc.	DC	113	Robco International Corporation	IL	38
Hockman Lewis Limited	NJ	57	Rodriguez, R.A., Inc.	NY	84
Holmes, Cecil Int'l Corp.	CA	7	Rusk International Corp.	CT	112
Hosler & Associates, Inc.	MO	50	San Pedro Products, Co.	FL	28
IBEX Technical Corp.	PA	100	Saria International, Inc.	CA	15
Imtrex Corporation	OH	93	Saris Corp.	WA	108
Industrial Engineering Int'l, Inc.	IL	34	Semsco International	FL	28
International Communications, Inc.	MA	115	Silo International, Inc.	NY	86
International Controls Co., Inc.	PA	100	Smythe International Services	CA	112
International Product Mktg. Group Inc.	CA	9	State Export Corporation	PA	101
International Purchasers	MD	43	Strato Enterprises	NJ	61
International Trades	CA	111	Sylvan Ginsbury Ltd.	NJ	61
Intertech Worldwide Corp.	FL	26	Symbicon Associates, Inc.	NH	53
Intrax	MA	46	Taurus Shipping & Trading Co.	OH	95
J & M Company, Ltd.	IL	35	Technic Group	TN	103
Kalamazoo International, Inc.	MI	48	Timcorp Int'l Marketing Co., Ltd.	HI	31
Karl, Peter A., International Sales	NY	79	Torning International, Inc.	CT	20
Kellogg International, Inc.	IL	35	Trade Com International Inc.	OH	95
Kewanee International, Inc.	NJ	59	Trade Development Corp. of Chicago	CA	16
Kimain Co.	OH	117	Tradelink, Inc.	ID	31
L & W Equipment Corporation	CA	9	United Export Corporation	IN	40
Latco International, Inc.	SC	102	United Gulf Services, Inc.	CA	17
Levinson, Samuel & Associates, Inc.	IL	114	USExport, Inc.	NY	88
McKim Group	MA	46	UTAC America Inc.	NY	88
McLean International Marketing, Inc.	WI	108	Vanguard Int'l Management Services	NY	90
Mercator Corporation	PA	101	Verde America, Inc.	NY	90
Midwestern Trading Corp.	IL	36	VIE International Inc.	CT	20
Mondo-Comm Int'l Ltd.	NJ	60	Wellesley International Corp.	MA	47
Nagro-Berry International	IN	39	Wiesman & Company, Inc.	AZ	1
New World Management, Inc.	NY	82	Wolfson, P. J. Co., Inc.	NY	91
Nikiforov, George, Inc.	NY	83	World-Trade Services, Inc.	OH	96
Orbis International, Ltd.	CA	12	Worldwide Exporters, Inc.	CA	18
Orion International & Company, Inc.	CO	19	Worldwide Trade Opportunities, Inc.	CA	18
Pathon Company	OH	95	XPORT, Port Authority Trading Co.	NY	91
Pegasus International Corp.	NJ	60	Yagi, S. Inc., dba Primex, Inc.	CA	18
Prestige U.S. Exports	FL	27	ZED Group, Inc.	MA	47

25. LIGHTING

A & S International Marketing Co., Inc.	NY	64	F. P. Intersales Corporation	FL	25
A B International	CA	1	Globelink Incorporated	TX	104
Amas International, Inc.	FL	22	Grable, John Exports, Inc.	FL	25
AME Matex Corp.	NJ	54	Hall & Reis, Inc.	NY	76
American Amenities, Inc.	CA	111	Hemisol Export & Import Corp.	FL	26
Ballagh & Thrall, Inc.	PA	98	Hosler & Associates, Inc.	MO	50
Boar's Head Int'l Trading Co.	WA	106	Intra-World Export Co., Inc.	NY	78
C. International	NJ	54	J & M Company, Ltd.	IL	35
Dunlap International	IA	40	Jajin Trading and Marketing, Inc.	WA	107
Electrical Sales Corp. Int'l	FL	24	JDRAS Enterprises, Inc.	NJ	58

Manhattan Nassau Corp.	NY	80
Meridian Group, The	CA	10
Natcom International	OH	94
Ohio Overseas Corporation	OH	94
Overseas Operations Inc.	CA	12
Quatro International, Inc.	FL	28
Roldan Products Corporation	MO	50
Romac Export Management Corp.	CA	14
Saria International, Inc.	CA	15

Silo International, Inc.	NY	86
Subent Co., Inc.	IL	38
TRADECO Association of N.Y., Ltd.	NY	87
Trans Tech Management Consulting	IL	115
UTAC America Inc.	NY	88
Wellesley International Corp.	MA	47
XPORT, Port Authority Trading Co.	NY	91
ZED Group, Inc.	MA	47

26. MACHINERY & SUPPLIES

Actrade International Corp.	NY	64
AGB International Management Corp.	NY	66
Alkier Consulting (Consult U.S.A., Inc.)	IL	114
Allied Systems Export Corp.	PA	97
Amex, Inc.	MN	49
Asia Marketing & Consulting Corp.	UT	105
Bauer, Alex & Co.	NJ	54
Berkowitz, N. C. & Company	CA	4
Borco Engineering Co.	WI	108
British-American Forfaiting Co., Inc.	MO	116
Browne International Industries, Inc.	NY	68
Caravan Export Corp.	NY	68
Engineering Equipment Co.	IL	33
EX-IM U.S.A., Inc.	IL	33
Export Procedures Co.	PA	99
Expotech	GA	30
Ferrex International, Inc.	NY	72
Fields International	IL	33
Fortune Enterprises International Co.	PA	100
G.D.E., Inc.	CA	5
H. L. Int'l Trade Advisors	MN	115
Hall & Reis, Inc.	NY	76
Hosler & Associates, Inc.	MO	50
Imtrex Corporation	OH	93
International Consolidated Exchange	OH	93
International ICS Group Inc.	CA	111
International Marketing Consultants	IL	34
International Purchasers	MD	43
Intertech Worldwide Corp.	FL	26
Intra-World Export Co., Inc.	NY	78
Intrax	MA	46
ISIS International Export Mgmt. Co.	UT	105
Jahn, Henry R. & Son, Inc.	NY	78
Kellogg International, Inc.	IL	35
Kimain Co.	OH	117
Klockner Ina Industrial Installations	NY	79
Latco International, Inc.	SC	102

Levinson, Samuel & Associates, Inc.	IL	114
Mancor	WA	119
McLean International Marketing, Inc.	WI	108
Midwest Agricultural Export Corp.	WI	108
Moss, Paul E. & Company Inc.	NY	82
Nagro-Berry International	IN	39
Nikiforov, George, Inc.	NY	83
Ohio Overseas Corporation	OH	94
Orbis International, Ltd.	CA	12
Pacific Exports	CA	13
Pegasus International Corp.	NJ	60
PNR International, Ltd.	IL	37
Protrade International	ME	42
Raba Corporation	HI	114
Rizzo, Joseph F. Company	AZ	1
Robb, R. Int'l Associates, Inc.	MI	49
Rodriguez, R.A., Inc.	NY	84
San Pedro Products, Co.	FL	28
Semsco International	FL	28
Silo International, Inc.	NY	86
Strato Enterprises	NJ	61
Sylvan Ginsbury Ltd.	NJ	61
Technic Group	TN	103
Tecnomaster Int'l Corp.	NJ	61
Tecnomasters International Corp.	NY	86
Timcorp Int'l Marketing Co., Ltd.	HI	31
Torning International, Inc.	CT	20
Trade Development Corp. of Chicago	CA	16
Tradex International, Inc.	CA	17
Turnkey Projects, Inc.	OR	118
Vanguard Int'l Management Services	NY	90
VIE International Inc.	CT	20
Wellesley International Corp.	MA	47
Wiesman & Company, Inc.	AZ	1
World-Trade Services, Inc.	OH	96
ZED Group, Inc.	MA	47

27. MEDICAL EQUIPMENT

Abaco International Corp.	CA	2	Honigberg, J. D., Int'l, Inc.	IL	34
Ad. Auriema Inc.	NY	66	IBEX Technical Corp.	PA	100
Alkier Consulting (Consult U.S.A., Inc.)	IL	114	IFRAS, Inc.	NY	77
Allied Systems Export Corp.	PA	97	Inter Euro Trading, Inc.	NY	78
Amed International	FL	22	Intercontinental Enterprises Ltd.	CA	9
Amerasia Trading Co., Inc.	CA	2	International Business Resources Inc.	HI	114
American Amenities, Inc.	CA	111	International Enterprises	TN	118
American Export Trading Co.	CA	2	International ICS Group Inc.	CA	111
American Trade International Corp.	UT	105	International Projects, Inc.	OH	93
Amex, Inc.	MN	49	Intertech Worldwide Corp.	FL	26
Amtrade International Corp.	CA	3	Intertrade Services, Inc.	NJ	116
ARC International Group, Inc.	MA	45	Intrax	MA	46
Atali-Mare, Ltd.	GA	29	ITBR, Inc.	TX	104
Bay World Trading, Ltd.	CA	4	ITM Corporation	DC	21
Berkowitz, N. C. & Company	CA	4	ITM Corporation	CA	112
Boar's Head Int'l Trading Co.	WA	106	JDRAS Enterprises, Inc.	NJ	58
Bock Pharmaceutical, Inc.	OH	92	Jireh International	PA	101
C. International	NJ	54	Medica International, Ltd.	IL	36
Camex International, Inc.	FL	23	Medical International, Inc.	NJ	59
Chicago Midwest Export Marketing	IL	32	Meridian Synapse Corp.	NY	81
Co-To Trading Corp.	NY	69	Minthorne Int'l Company	NY	81
Cobble Hill International	MA	45	New World Management, Inc.	NY	82
CPS Marketing Corp.	FL	23	Ohio Overseas Corporation	OH	94
Creative International, Inc.	NJ	55	Onyx Enterprises, Inc.	NY	83
Curtis TradeGroup, Inc.	IN	38	Orbis International, Ltd.	CA	12
Davis Elliott International Inc.	PA	98	Orion International & Company, Inc.	CO	19
Debco Chemicals Sales, Co.	NY	70	Pan Pacific International	CA	13
Dosik International	MD	43	Pegasus International Corp.	NJ	60
Dunlap Export Co., Inc.	OH	92	Prestige U.S. Exports	FL	27
Dunlap International	IA	40	Products Corp. of North America, Inc.	OR	97
Dynacon	MO	50	Protrade International	ME	42
E & G International, Inc.	FL	24	Quatro International, Inc.	FL	28
Eagle International Enterprises, Inc.	CA	5	Quest International	HI	31
Electrical Manufacturers Export Co.	ME	42	Rajiv International, Inc.	MD	44
Empire Equities Inc.	NY	72	RHA Group	CA	14
ERW International Inc.	IL	33	Rodriguez, R.A., Inc.	NY	84
Euroscand, Inc.	FL	24	Roldan Products Corporation	MO	50
Ewig, Carl F. Inc.	NJ	56	Rusk International Corp.	CT	112
Expomar International Inc.	NJ	56	Schwanke Int'l Marketing Corp.	IN	40
Expotech	GA	30	Sharoubim International Group, Inc.	NY	84
Fernandez Import/Export, Inc. USA	NC	50	Silo International, Inc.	NY	86
First Gulf International, Inc.	TX	104	Skyex Inc.	FL	29
Fremont Group Limited	IL	114	Smythe International Services	CA	112
Gas International Corp., The	NJ	57	Strong Trading Company	NH	53
Gladex Corporation	CA	6	Symbicon Associates, Inc.	NH	53
Global Dimensions Corp.	TX	118	T A International, Inc.	CA	16
Global Marketing Concepts	NC	52	Technic Group	TN	103
Glynn International, Inc.	MA	46	Trade Development Corp. of Chicago	CA	16
HCI Corporation	VA	106	Tradelink, Inc.	ID	31

Tradex International	OH	96	Viking Traders Inc.	NJ	62
Tradex International, Inc.	CA	17	Wellesley International Corp.	MA	47
Trans Tech Management Consulting	IL	115	Winters, J.C. Company	NJ	62
Tratech International, Inc.	AL	111	Witz Scientific, Inc.	OH	96
U.S. Export Marketing Group	NY	88	World-Trade Services, Inc.	OH	96
United Exporters Co.	CA	17	Worldwide Trade Opportunities, Inc.	CA	18
United Exporters Service, Inc.	KY	41	XPORT, Port Authority Trading Co.	NY	91
UTAC America Inc.	NY	88			

28. MARINE & RELATED PRODUCTS

Amas International, Inc.	FL	22	International Projects, Inc.	OH	93
American Export Trading Co.	CA	2	International Trades	CA	111
American Industrial Export Ltd.	NY	66	ISIS International Export Mgmt. Co.	UT	105
Amtrade International Corp.	CA	3	Items Unlimited	NJ	116
Anaheim Marketing International	CA	3	Kato International, Inc.	NJ	58
Berkowitz, N. C. & Company	CA	4	Minthorne Int'l Company	NY	81
Bisho, J. R. Co., Inc.	CA	4	New World Management, Inc.	NY	82
C.C.I., Inc.	IL	32	Pacific Export Services, Inc.	TX	105
Charon-Jessam Trading Co. Inc.	NY	69	Quest International	HI	31
Dreyco, Inc.	NJ	55	Romac Export Management Corp.	CA	14
Ewig, Carl F. Inc.	NJ	56	Row International, Inc.	CA	15
EX-IM U.S.A., Inc.	IL	33	Sharoubim International Group, Inc.	NY	84
Gladex Corporation	CA	6	Silo International, Inc.	NY	86
Gomez, Manuel and Associates, Inc.	FL	25	Taico Trading Corporation	CA	16
Hall & Reis, Inc.	NY	76	Technic Group	TN	103
High Technology Export Services, Inc.	DC	113	Trade Management Services	MN	49
IFRAS, Inc.	NY	77	United Exporters Co.	CA	17
International Business Resources Inc.	HI	114	Wiesman & Company, Inc.	AZ	1
International ICS Group Inc.	CA	111	Wolfson, P. J. Co., Inc.	NY	91
International Product Mktg. Group Inc.	CA	9			

29. MATERIALS HANDLING EQUIPMENT

AEON International Corp.	IA	40	G.D.E., Inc.	CA	5
AmTrade Aid, Inc.	NJ	116	Globelink Incorporated	TX	104
Aztek International Corp.	IN	38	Gregg Company, Ltd., The	NJ	57
Ballagh & Thrall, Inc.	PA	98	Hall & Reis, Inc.	NY	76
Berkowitz, N. C. & Company	CA	4	Holmes, Cecil Int'l Corp.	CA	7
Bisho, J. R. Co., Inc.	CA	4	International Purchasers	MD	43
British-American Forfaiting Co., Inc.	MO	116	Intertech Worldwide Corp.	FL	26
Domestic & International Technology	PA	98	Jahn, Henry R. & Son, Inc.	NY	78
Dorian America	NY	70	Kallman Associates	NJ	117
Dunlap International	IA	40	Klockner Ina Industrial Installations	NY	79
Engineering Equipment Co.	IL	33	Latco International, Inc.	SC	102
ERW International Inc.	IL	33	McKim Group	MA	46
Far East Trade & Investment Co.	PA	99	Mercator Corporation	PA	101
Fields International	IL	33	Pegasus International Corp.	NJ	60
First Gulf International, Inc.	TX	104	Pennvint	NJ	60
Fremont Group Limited	IL	114	PNR International, Ltd.	IL	37

Prestige U.S. Exports	FL	27	Tecnomaster Int'l Corp.	NJ	61
Protrade International	ME	42	Timcorp Int'l Marketing Co., Ltd.	HI	31
San Pedro Products, Co.	FL	28	Tradex International	OH	96
Sharoubim International Group, Inc.	NY	84	USExport, Inc.	NY	88
Silo International, Inc.	NY	86	Wiesman & Company, Inc.	AZ	1
Technic Group	TN	103			

30. MINING EQUIPMENT, MINERALS & RAW MATERIALS

Ad. Auriema Inc.	NY	66	Intertrade Services, Inc.	NJ	116
AGB International Management Corp.	NY	66	ISIS International Export Mgmt. Co.	UT	105
Amerasia Trading Co., Inc.	CA	2	ITBR, Inc.	TX	104
American Export Trading Co.	CA	2	Jahn, Henry R. & Son, Inc.	NY	78
AmTrade Aid, Inc.	NJ	116	Kallman Associates	NJ	117
Automotive International Corp.	TX	103	Kato International, Inc.	NJ	58
Bisho, J. R. Co., Inc.	CA	4	Klockner Ina Industrial Installations	NY	79
British-American Forfaiting Co., Inc.	MO	116	MK Technology/Deltac	DC	113
Chaco International, Inc.	CA	5	Morse Agri-Energy Associates	CA	112
Chicago Midwest Export Marketing	IL	32	New Mexico Int'l Trade & Devel. Co.	NM	62
Debco Chemicals Sales, Co.	NY	70	New World Management, Inc.	NY	82
Domestic & International Technology	PA	98	Orbis International, Ltd.	CA	12
Dynacon	MO	50	Orion International & Company, Inc.	CO	19
Eagle International Enterprises, Inc.	CA	5	Protrade International	ME	42
Expotech	GA	30	Provident Traders, Inc.	CA	13
Ferrex International, Inc.	NY	72	Reed, Charles H. Export, Inc.	MA	46
FWD International, Inc.	IL	34	San Pedro Products, Co.	FL	28
Gladex Corporation	CA	6	Tecnomaster Int'l Corp.	NJ	61
Gregg Company, Ltd., The	NJ	57	Tradex International, Inc.	CA	17
Hall & Reis, Inc.	NY	76	VIE International Inc.	CT	20
Holmes, Cecil Int'l Corp.	CA	7	Wiesman & Company, Inc.	AZ	1
Imtrex Corporation	OH	93	Wolfson, P. J. Co., Inc.	NY	91
Inter Euro Trading, Inc.	NY	78	Yagi, S. Inc., dba Primex, Inc.	CA	18
International Purchasers	MD	43			

31. OPTICAL, PHOTO, SCIENTIFIC INSTRUMENTS

A & S International Marketing Co., Inc.	NY	64	Global Marketing Services, Inc.	FL	25
Allied Systems Export Corp.	PA	97	High Technology Export Services, Inc.	DC	113
Avalon Group, Ltd.	CA	4	IBEX Technical Corp.	PA	100
Ballagh & Thrall, Inc.	PA	98	IMEX Trading, Ltd.	CA	8
Centrex, Inc.	NY	69	Intercontinental Enterprises Ltd.	CA	9
Chicago Import/Export Consultants	IL	114	International Business Resources Inc.	HI	114
Co-To Trading Corp.	NY	69	International Controls Co., Inc.	PA	100
Cobble Hill International	MA	45	Intra-World Export Co., Inc.	NY	78
Debco Chemicals Sales, Co.	NY	70	Intrax	MA	46
Dosik International	MD	43	Kammeh Int'l Trade Co.	IL	35
Ewig, Carl F. Inc.	NJ	56	Lotus Group, The	NC	52
Export Consultant Service	PA	98	Mancor	WA	119
First Gulf International, Inc.	TX	104	Meridian Synapse Corp.	NY	81
Gilman Industrial Exports, Inc.	NY	74	Midwestern Trading Corp.	IL	36

Minthorne Int'l Company	NY	81	Trade Development Corp. of Chicago	CA	16
MK Technology/Deltac	DC	113	Tratech International, Inc.	AL	111
Ohio Overseas Corporation	OH	94	United Gulf Services, Inc.	CA	17
Regalis USA, Inc.	CA	14	UTAC America Inc.	NY	88
Rodriguez, R.A., Inc.	NY	84	Wellesley International Corp.	MA	47
Roldan Products Corporation	MO	50	Witz Scientific, Inc.	OH	96
Sacks, Harvey C. Export Consulting	CA	15	Worldwide Exporters, Inc.	CA	18
Sylvan Ginsbury Ltd.	NJ	61	ZED Group, Inc.	MA	47

32. PAINTS, VARNISHES & ENAMELS

A B International	CA	1	Lotus Group, The	NC	52
Akron Overseas Inc.	OH	92	Natcom International	OH	94
AME Matex Corp.	NJ	54	Ohio Overseas Corporation	OH	94
American Amenities, Inc.	CA	111	Pegasus International Corp.	NJ	60
Avalon Group, Ltd.	CA	4	Prior, John Inc.	NY	83
Ballagh & Thrall, Inc.	PA	98	Rivard International Corp.	OH	95
Celestial Mercantile Corp.	NY	68	Saria International, Inc.	CA	15
Chemical Export Company, Inc.	MA	45	Trade Com International Inc.	OH	95
Davis Elliott International Inc.	PA	98	United Gulf Services, Inc.	CA	17
Debco Chemicals Sales, Co.	NY	70	VIE International Inc.	CT	20
Grable, John Exports, Inc.	FL	25	Wiesman & Company, Inc.	AZ	1
Import Export Management Svc., Inc.	TX	104	Worldwide Trade Opportunities, Inc.	CA	18
International Product Mktg. Group Inc.	CA	9	Yagi, S. Inc., dba Primex, Inc.	CA	18
Intra-World Export Co., Inc.	NY	78			

33. PAPER, PACKAGING & CONTAINERS

Actrade International Corp.	NY	64	Kalamazoo International, Inc.	MI	48
Amas International, Inc.	FL	22	Kammeh Int'l Trade Co.	IL	35
C. International	NJ	54	Lanla Sales	NY	80
Chew International	NY	69	Matthews Globus Trading, Ltd.	PA	101
Dunlap International	IA	40	Morse Agri-Energy Associates	CA	112
Ewig, Carl F. Inc.	NJ	56	Nagro-Berry International	IN	39
Export Trade of America, Inc.	NY	72	Natcom International	OH	94
Grand Pacific Finance Corp.	NY	74	New Mexico Int'l Trade & Devel. Co.	NM	62
Import Export Management Svc., Inc.	TX	104	Products Corp. of North America, Inc.	OR	97
International Trades	CA	111	Reed, Charles H. Export, Inc.	MA	46
Intra-World Export Co., Inc.	NY	78	Rusk International Corp.	CT	112
ISIS International Export Mgmt. Co.	UT	105	Timcorp Int'l Marketing Co., Ltd.	HI	31
ITBR, Inc.	TX	104	Tradex International	OH	96
ITM Corporation	CA	112	Vanguard Int'l Management Services	NY	90
Jajin Trading and Marketing, Inc.	WA	107	VIE International Inc.	CT	20

34. PHARMACEUTICALS & HOSPITAL SUPPLIES

Allied Systems Export Corp.	PA	97	International Business Resources Inc.	HI	114
Amerasia Trading Co., Inc.	CA	2	International Enterprises	TN	118
American Export Trading Co.	CA	2	ITM Corporation	CA	112
Anaheim Marketing International	CA	3	ITM Corporation	DC	21
ARC International Group, Inc.	MA	45	Kato International, Inc.	NJ	58
Atali-Mare, Ltd.	GA	29	Lotus Group, The	NC	52
Bay World Trading, Ltd.	CA	4	Medica International, Ltd.	IL	36
Bock Pharmaceutical, Inc.	OH	92	Medical International, Inc.	NJ	59
C. International	NJ	54	Meridian Synapse Corp.	NY	81
Camex International, Inc.	FL	23	Mirage Products International, Inc.	CA	11
Caravan Export Corp.	NY	68	Mondo-Comm Int'l Ltd.	NJ	60
Celestial Mercantile Corp.	NY	68	Muni Trading Co., Inc.	NJ	60
Chemical Export Company, Inc.	MA	45	Ohio Overseas Corporation	OH	94
Chihade International, Inc.	GA	29	Onyx Enterprises, Inc.	NY	83
Co-To Trading Corp.	NY	69	Pan Pacific International	CA	13
CPS Marketing Corp.	FL	23	Pegasus International Corp.	NJ	60
Creative International, Inc.	NJ	55	Products Corp. of North America, Inc.	OR	97
Davidson International	NJ	55	Protrade International	ME	42
Davis Elliott International Inc.	PA	98	Quatro International, Inc.	FL	28
Dunlap Export Co., Inc.	OH	92	Quest International	HI	31
Dunlap International	IA	40	Raba Corporation	HI	114
Dynacon	MO	50	Regalis USA, Inc.	CA	14
Eagle International Enterprises, Inc.	CA	5	Sharoubim International Group, Inc.	NY	84
Empire Equities Inc.	NY	72	T A International, Inc.	CA	16
ERW International Inc.	IL	33	Trade Com International Inc.	OH	95
Expomar International Inc.	NJ	56	Tradelink, Inc.	ID	31
Fernandez Import/Export, Inc. USA	NC	50	Tradex International	OH	96
First Gulf International, Inc.	TX	104	Tratech International, Inc.	AL	111
Gas International Corp., The	NJ	57	United Exporters Service, Inc.	KY	41
Global Dimensions Corp.	TX	118	Winters, J.C. Company	NJ	62
Glynn International, Inc.	MA	46	Witz Scientific, Inc.	OH	96
Hardy, M. W. & Co, Inc.	NY	76	World-Trade Services, Inc.	OH	96
Imtrex Corporation	OH	93	Worldwide Trade Opportunities, Inc.	CA	18
Intercontinental Enterprises Ltd.	CA	9	XPORT, Port Authority Trading Co.	NY	91

35. PUBLIC UTILITIES

Amas International, Inc.	FL	22	Quatro International, Inc.	FL	28
Engineering Equipment Co.	IL	33	Wellesley International Corp.	MA	47
Gladex Corporation	CA	6			

36. RESTAURANT, HOTEL & CATERING EQUIPMENT

A & S International Marketing Co., Inc.	NY	64	Anaheim Marketing International	CA	3
Actrade International Corp.	NY	64	BMIL International	NY	67
Ad. Auriema Inc.	NY	66	Boar's Head Int'l Trading Co.	WA	106
Alkier Consulting (Consult U.S.A., Inc.)	IL	114	Bryan, Errol H. International	NY	68
AME Matex Corp.	NJ	54	Chihade International, Inc.	GA	29
American Amenities, Inc.	CA	111	Cobo, J. & Associates, Inc.	FL	23

CPS Marketing Corp.	FL	23	Intra-World Export Co., Inc.	NY	78
Domestic & International Technology	PA	98	ITBR, Inc.	TX	104
Dorian America	NY	70	ITM Corporation	CA	112
Dunlap International	IA	40	Kalglas International Inc.	NY	79
Electrical Sales Corp. Int'l	FL	24	Kallman Associates	NJ	117
Ewig, Carl F. Inc.	NJ	56	Kammeh Int'l Trade Co.	IL	35
Exmart International, Inc.	NJ	56	Klockner Ina Industrial Installations	NY	79
Fernandez Import/Export, Inc. USA	NC	50	LKS International	IL	35
Fields International	IL	33	Manhattan Nassau Corp.	NY	80
Fleetwood International	NY	73	Medica International, Ltd.	IL	36
Geonex International Corp.	NY	74	Nikiforov, George, Inc.	NY	83
Gladex Corporation	CA	6	Ohio Overseas Corporation	OH	94
Globelink Incorporated	TX	104	Prior, John Inc.	NY	83
Hemisol Export & Import Corp.	FL	26	Protrade International	ME	42
Honigberg, J. D., Int'l, Inc.	IL	34	Quatro International, Inc.	FL	28
Horn, John Stanley Co., Inc.	CA	7	Regalis USA, Inc.	CA	14
Inter-America Sales Co., Inc.	LA	42	Roldan Products Corporation	MO	50
International Consolidated Exchange	OH	93	Romac Export Management Corp.	CA	14
International Enterprises	TN	118	Sheldon, H.D. & Company, Inc.	NY	86
International Projects, Inc.	OH	93	Wolfson, P. J. Co., Inc.	NY	91
Intertech Worldwide Corp.	FL	26			

37. SAFETY & SECURITY EQUIPMENT

313 R/E Ltd.	NY	64	Intercontinental Enterprises Ltd.	CA	9
A & S International Marketing Co., Inc.	NY	64	International Trades	CA	111
Allied Systems Export Corp.	PA	97	Intrax	MA	46
American Amenities, Inc.	CA	111	ITBR, Inc.	TX	104
American Export Trading Co.	CA	2	ITM Corporation	CA	112
American Industrial Export Ltd.	NY	66	Kalamazoo International, Inc.	MI	48
ARC International Group, Inc.	MA	45	M & P Export Management Corp.	NJ	59
Avalon Group, Ltd.	CA	4	McLean International Marketing, Inc.	WI	108
Ballagh & Thrall, Inc.	PA	98	Mirage Products International, Inc.	CA	11
Beijing Trade Exchange, Inc.	DC	21	Multimart Corporation	GA	30
Bogart International Sales	OH	92	Nesa Corporation	CT	20
Camex International, Inc.	FL	23	New Mexico Int'l Trade & Devel. Co.	NM	62
Da Miano & Graham Ltd.	IL	32	Ohio Overseas Corporation	OH	94
Davis Elliott International Inc.	PA	98	Onyx Enterprises, Inc.	NY	83
Domestic & International Technology	PA	98	Overseas Operations Inc.	CA	12
Donovan, W. J. Co.	NY	70	Quatro International, Inc.	FL	28
Engineering Equipment Co.	IL	33	Quest International	HI	31
ERW International Inc.	IL	33	RKF International Inc.	IL	37
Exportus Ltd.	MD	43	Romac Export Management Corp.	CA	14
Fernandez Import/Export, Inc. USA	NC	50	Saria International, Inc.	CA	15
Ferrex International, Inc.	NY	72	Silo International, Inc.	NY	86
Frontier Trading	CA	111	Skyex Inc.	FL	29
Grand Pacific Finance Corp.	NY	74	Trade Management Services	MN	49
Hall & Reis, Inc.	NY	76	TRADECO Association of N.Y., Ltd.	NY	87
Hallmarkets International, Ltd.	NY	76	United Export Corporation	IN	40
Halprin International	CA	6	United Exporters Service, Inc.	KY	41
Hypron, Inc.	CA	8	United Gulf Services, Inc.	CA	17

UTAC America Inc.	NY	88	Wiesman & Company, Inc.	AZ	1
Verde America, Inc.	NY	90	Witz Scientific, Inc.	OH	96
VIE International Inc.	CT	20	World-Trade Services, Inc.	OH	96
Wellesley International Corp.	MA	47	Worldwide Trade Opportunities, Inc.	CA	18

38. SPORTING GOODS

Abaco International Corp.	CA	2	Intra-World Export Co., Inc.	NY	78
Alkier Consulting (Consult U.S.A., Inc.)	IL	114	Items Unlimited	NJ	116
AME Matex Corp.	NJ	54	ITM Corporation	CA	112
American Amenities, Inc.	CA	111	J & M Company, Ltd.	IL	35
Amtrade International Corp.	CA	3	Kammeh Int'l Trade Co.	IL	35
Beijing Trade Exchange, Inc.	DC	21	Kimain Co.	OH	117
Bogart International Sales	OH	92	Levinson, Samuel & Associates, Inc.	IL	114
C. International	NJ	54	Lotus Group, The	NC	52
Celestial Mercantile Corp.	NY	68	Moran's International Services	ME	42
Cobble Hill International	MA	45	Pacific Export Services, Inc.	TX	105
Davidson International	NJ	55	Piedmont Caribbean Trade Limited	NC	52
Dreyco, Inc.	NJ	55	Protrade International	ME	42
Dunlap International	IA	40	Quest International	HI	31
E & G International, Inc.	FL	24	Reed, Charles H. Export, Inc.	MA	46
Embree, C. A. Co.	TN	102	Regalis USA, Inc.	CA	14
Euroscand, Inc.	FL	24	RKF International Inc.	IL	37
EX-IM U.S.A., Inc.	IL	33	Romac Export Management Corp.	CA	14
Export Trade of America, Inc.	NY	72	Strong Trading Company	NH	53
Gas International Corp., The	NJ	57	Taico Trading Corporation	CA	16
Global Merchandising Corp.	CA	6	Trade Management Services	MN	49
Hall & Reis, Inc.	NY	76	TRADECO Association of N.Y., Ltd.	NY	87
Heritage International Inc.	CA	7	Tradelink, Inc.	ID	31
Inter Euro Trading, Inc.	NY	78	United Export Corporation	IN	40
Intercontinental Enterprises Ltd.	CA	9	Universial Export Agencies	NY	88
International ICS Group Inc.	CA	111	USExport, Inc.	NY	88
International Marketing Consultants	IL	34	UTAC America Inc.	NY	88
International Product Mktg. Group Inc.	CA	9	Viking Traders Inc.	NJ	62
International Projects, Inc.	OH	93	Wellesley International Corp.	MA	47
Intertrade, Inc.	MI	48	Worldwide Trade Opportunities, Inc.	CA	18

39. TIME RECORDERS & SYSTEMS

Amas International, Inc.	FL	22	M. S. Universal, Inc.	NJ	59
Ballagh & Thrall, Inc.	PA	98	Ohio Overseas Corporation	OH	94
Boar's Head Int'l Trading Co.	WA	106	Pacific Export Services, Inc.	TX	105
Ewig, Carl F. Inc.	NJ	56	Quatro International, Inc.	FL	28
Hallmarkets International, Ltd.	NY	76	Silo International, Inc.	NY	86
Hypron, Inc.	CA	8	Wellesley International Corp.	MA	47
IBEX Technical Corp.	PA	100			

40. TESTING EQUIPMENT

A & S International Marketing Co., Inc.	NY	64	International Product Mktg. Group Inc.	CA	9
Allied Systems Export Corp.	PA	97	Intrax	MA	46
Amex, Inc.	MN	49	Lotus Group, The	NC	52
Avalon Group, Ltd.	CA	4	Mancor	WA	119
Ballagh & Thrall, Inc.	PA	98	Midwestern Trading Corp.	IL	36
Berkowitz, N. C. & Company	CA	4	MK Technology/Deltac	DC	113
Borco Engineering Co.	WI	108	Nagro-Berry International	IN	39
Caravan Export Corp.	NY	68	PNR International, Ltd.	IL	37
Chicago Import/Export Consultants	IL	114	Rodriguez, R.A., Inc.	NY	84
Co-To Trading Corp.	NY	69	Row International, Inc.	CA	15
Cobble Hill International	MA	45	Rusk International Corp.	CT	112
Da Miano & Graham Ltd.	IL	32	Sacks, Harvey C. Export Consulting	CA	15
Dage Corporation	CT	19	Sharoubim International Group, Inc.	NY	84
Domestic & International Technology	PA	98	Silicon International	CA	16
Ewig, Carl F. Inc.	NJ	56	Smythe International Services	CA	112
Exmart International, Inc.	NJ	56	Strato Enterprises	NJ	61
G.D.E., Inc.	CA	5	Surel International, Inc.	MA	47
Gladex Corporation	CA	6	Timcorp Int'l Marketing Co., Ltd.	HI	31
Global Merchandising Corp.	CA	6	Trade Development Corp. of Chicago	CA	16
Glynn International, Inc.	MA	46	Tradeways, Ltd.	VA	106
High Technology Export Services, Inc.	DC	113	Tradex International	OH	96
IBEX Technical Corp.	PA	100	United Exporters Co.	CA	17
IMEX Trading, Ltd.	CA	8	United Gulf Services, Inc.	CA	17
Intercontinental Enterprises Ltd.	CA	9	Wellesley International Corp.	MA	47
International Controls Co., Inc.	PA	100	Worldwide Exporters, Inc.	CA	18
International Marketing Consultants	IL	34			

41. TRUCKS, ACCESSORIES OR PARTS

American Export Trading Co.	CA	2	Duromotive Industries, Inc.	NY	71
Amex, Inc.	MN	49	Dynacon	MO	50
Asia Minor Export Import Co., Inc.	NJ	54	Eagle International Enterprises, Inc.	CA	5
Atlas Asia-Pacific	CA	3	Engineering Equipment Co.	IL	33
Automotive Export Inc.	FL	22	ERW International Inc.	IL	33
Automotive International Corp.	TX	103	Expomar International Inc.	NJ	56
Bisho, J. R. Co., Inc.	CA	4	Fernandez Import/Export, Inc. USA	NC	50
Bogart International Sales	OH	92	Fields International	IL	33
C.C.I., Inc.	IL	32	FWD International, Inc.	IL	34
Caravan Export Corp.	NY	68	Geon International Corp.	IN	39
Celestial Mercantile Corp.	NY	68	Gladex Corporation	CA	6
Charon-Jessam Trading Co. Inc.	NY	69	Gomez, Manuel and Associates, Inc.	FL	25
Chazen Industrial Corp.	NJ	55	Grand Pacific Finance Corp.	NY	74
Chicago Import/Export Consultants	IL	114	Hayden, Inc.	CA	7
Colonial International Corp.- COINCO	FL	23	Hemisol Export & Import Corp.	FL	26
Detroit Parts Mfg. Co.	MI	48	International Product Mktg. Group Inc.	CA	9
Domestic & International Technology	PA	98	Intraco Corporation	MI	48
Drake America	NY	71	Iowa Export Import Trading Co.	IA	41
Dreyco, Inc.	NJ	55	ITBR, Inc.	TX	104
Dunlap Export Co., Inc.	OH	92	ITM Corporation	CA	112
Dunlap International	IA	40	J & M Sales Corporation	NJ	58

Kammeh Int'l Trade Co.	IL	35	Rodriguez, R.A., Inc.	NY	84
Liberty Automotive Inc.	NY	80	San Pedro Products, Co.	FL	28
Lindeco International Corp.	FL	27	Schwanke Int'l Marketing Corp.	IN	40
M. S. Universal, Inc.	NJ	59	Spivey, James S., Inc.	MD	44
Magna Automotive Industries	NY	80	Taurus Shipping & Trading Co.	OH	95
Midwestern Trading Corp.	IL	36	Teleport Corporation	NJ	61
Morris Bros. Auto Trucks & Parts Corp.	NY	82	VIE International Inc.	CT	20
Motorex Sales Corp.	NY	82	Wolfson, P. J. Co., Inc.	NY	91
Orbis International, Ltd.	CA	12	Worldwide Trade Opportunities, Inc.	CA	18
Prior, John Inc.	NY	83	Yagi, S. Inc., dba Primex, Inc.	CA	18
Regalis USA, Inc.	CA	14	Zeller World Trade Corp.	OH	96
Rivard International Corp.	OH	95			

ALPHABETICAL INDEX OF EXPORT MANAGEMENT COMPANIES

Dorian America	NY	70	Gerson International Corp.	IN	39
Dosik International	MD	43	Gibbons, J.T., Inc.	LA	41
Drake America	NY	71	Gilman Industrial Exports, Inc.	NY	74
Dreyco, Inc.	NJ	55	Gladex Corporation	CA	6
Dreyfus & Associates, Ltd.	NY	71	Global Marketing Concepts	NC	52
Dunlap Export Co., Inc.	OH	92	Global Marketing Services, Inc.	FL	25
Dunlap International	IA	40	Global Merchandising Corp.	CA	6
Duromotive Industries, Inc.	NY	71	Global Technology, Inc.	CA	6
Dynacon	MO	50	Globelink Incorporated	TX	104
E & G International, Inc.	FL	24	Glynn International, Inc.	MA	46
Eagle International Enterprises, Inc.	CA	5	Gomez, Manuel and Associates, Inc.	FL	25
Electrical Manufacturers Export Co.	ME	42	Grable, John Exports, Inc.	FL	25
Electrical Sales Corp. Int'l	FL	24	Grand Pacific Finance Corp.	NY	74
Elmi Inc.	NY	71	Gregg Company, Ltd., The	NJ	57
EMB Trading Co.	NY	72	Hall & Reis, Inc.	NY	76
Embree, C. A. Co.	TN	102	Haller, Mart Inc.	FL	26
Empire Equities Inc.	NY	72	Hallmarkets International, Ltd.	NY	76
Engineering Equipment Co.	IL	33	Halprin International	CA	6
ERW International Inc.	IL	33	Handforth Company, The	PA	100
Euroscand, Inc.	FL	24	Hardy, M. W. & Co, Inc.	NY	76
Ewig, Carl F. Inc.	NJ	56	Hayden, Inc.	CA	7
EX-IM U.S.A., Inc.	IL	33	HCI Corporation	VA	106
Exmart International, Inc.	NJ	56	Hemisol Export & Import Corp.	FL	26
Expo International Co., Inc.	NJ	56	Heritage International Inc.	CA	7
Expomar International Inc.	NJ	56	Hockman Lewis Limited	NJ	57
Export Agencies Int'l Corp.	IN	39	Hoffman International, Inc.	NJ	58
Export Consultant Service	PA	98	Holmes, Cecil Int'l Corp.	CA	7
Export Procedures Co.	PA	99	Honigberg, J. D., Int'l, Inc.	IL	34
Export Trade of America, Inc.	NY	72	Horn, John Stanley Co., Inc.	CA	7
Exportus Ltd.	MD	43	Hosler & Associates, Inc.	MO	50
Expotech	GA	30	Hyman, Harry & Son, Inc.	NY	76
Express Parts	OH	93	Hypron, Inc.	CA	8
F. P. Intersales Corporation	FL	25	IBEX Technical Corp.	PA	100
Fairco, Inc.	LA	41	IFRAS, Inc.	NY	77
Fame International	TX	103	IMEX Trading, Ltd.	CA	8
Far East Trade & Investment Co.	PA	99	Import Export Management Svc., Inc.	TX	104
Fernandez Import/Export, Inc. USA	NC	50	Imtrex Corporation	OH	93
Ferrex International, Inc.	NY	72	Indamerica International, Inc.	CA	8
Fields International	IL	33	Industrial Engineering Int'l, Inc.	IL	34
First Gulf International, Inc.	TX	104	INEX International	CA	8
Fischer Enterprises Inc.	NY	73	INEX Technology International	MD	43
Fleetwood International	NY	73	INSECO, Inc.	NY	77
FMI Automotive Corp./FMI Trading	NY	73	Inter Euro Trading, Inc.	NY	78
Fortune Enterprises International Co.	PA	100	Inter-America Sales Co., Inc.	LA	42
FWD International, Inc.	IL	34	Intercontinental Enterprises Ltd.	CA	9
G.D.E., Inc.	CA	5	International Computer Systems	CA	9
Gas International Corp., The	NJ	57	International Consolidated Exchange	OH	93
Gate Group U.S.A., Inc.	NY	73	International Controls Co., Inc.	PA	100
General Product Co., Inc.	NJ	57	International Industries Corp.	SC	102
Geon International Corp.	IN	39	International Marketing Consultants	IL	34
Geonex International Corp.	NY	74	International Marketing Services Co.	WA	107
Gerber, J. & Co., Inc.	NY	74	International Marketing Systems, Ltd.	ND	52

Provident Traders, Inc.	CA	13	Tecnomaster Int'l Corp.	NJ	61
Proxima Inc.	NY	84	Tecnomasters International Corp.	NY	86
Quatro International, Inc.	FL	28	Teleport Corporation	NJ	61
Quest International	HI	31	Third Party International	OR	97
Rajiv International, Inc.	MD	44	Timcorp Int'l Marketing Co., Ltd.	HI	31
Rebel, Albert & Associates, Inc.	CA	14	Torning International, Inc.	CT	20
Reed, Charles H. Export, Inc.	MA	46	Trade Development Corp. of Chicago	CA	16
Regalis USA, Inc.	CA	14	Trade Management Services	MN	49
Rexton Corp.	FL	28	TRADECO Association of N.Y., Ltd.	NY	87
RHA Group	CA	14	TradeCom International Inc.	OH	95
Rivard International Corp.	OH	95	Tradelink, Inc.	ID	31
Rizzo, Joseph F. Company	AZ	1	Tradeways, Ltd.	VA	106
RKF International Inc.	IL	37	Tradex International	OH	96
Robb, R. Int'l Associates, Inc.	MI	49	Tradex International, Inc.	CA	17
Robco International Corporation	IL	38	Trans International Group Ltd.	PA	102
Roburn Agencies Inc.	NY	84	Triple Gold Trading Inc.	CA	17
Rocky Mountain Export Co., Inc.	CO	19	TWT International	OR	97
Rodriguez, R.A., Inc.	NY	84	U.S. Export Marketing Group	NY	88
Roldan Products Corporation	MO	50	Ultramar Agencies Co.	NY	87
Romac Export Management Corp.	CA	14	United Export Corporation	IN	40
Row International, Inc.	CA	15	United Exporters Co.	CA	17
Sacks, Harvey C. Export Consulting	CA	15	United Exporters Service, Inc.	KY	41
San Pedro Products, Co.	FL	28	United Gulf Services, Inc.	CA	17
Saria International, Inc.	CA	15	United International Marketing Corp.	NJ	62
Saris Corp.	WA	108	Universal Data Consultants, Inc.	GA	31
Schmid, H. P. Inc.	CA	15	Universial Export Agencies	NY	88
Schwanke Int'l Marketing Corp.	IN	40	USExport, Inc.	NY	88
Semsco International	FL	28	UTAC America Inc.	NY	88
Sharoubim International Group, Inc.	NY	84	Vanguard Int'l Management Services	NY	90
Sheldon, H.D. & Company, Inc.	NY	86	Vensamar Export Management	AL	1
Sibco, Inc.	CT	20	Verde America, Inc.	NY	90
Silicon International	CA	16	VIE International Inc.	CT	20
Silo International, Inc.	NY	86	Viking Traders Inc.	NJ	62
Skyex Inc.	FL	29	Wedeen, Philip	NY	90
Software Export Corp.	MA	47	Wellesley International Corp.	MA	47
Sosin International, Inc.	GA	30	Whittaker, Benjamin Inc.	NY	90
Spivey, James S., Inc.	MD	44	Wiesman & Company, Inc.	AZ	1
State Export Corporation	PA	101	Winters, J.C. Company	NJ	62
Sterling International Corp.	NY	86	Witz Scientific, Inc.	OH	96
Strato Enterprises	NJ	61	Wolfson, P. J. Co., Inc.	NY	91
Strong Trading Company	NH	53	World-Trade Services, Inc.	OH	96
Subent Co., Inc.	IL	38	Worldwide Exporters, Inc.	CA	18
Surel International, Inc.	MA	47	Worldwide Trade Opportunities, Inc.	CA	18
Sylvan Ginsbury Ltd.	NJ	61	XPORT, Port Authority Trading Co.	NY	91
Symbicon Associates, Inc.	NH	53	Yagi, S. Inc., dba Primex, Inc.	CA	18
T A International, Inc.	CA	16	ZED Group, Inc.	MA	47
Taico Trading Corporation	CA	16	Zeller World Trade Corp.	OH	96
Taurus Shipping & Trading Co.	OH	95	Ziegler Corporation, The	CA	18
TechBridge Marketing	GA	30	Zuniga International	FL	29
Technic Group	TN	103			

ALPHABETICAL INDEX OF CONSULTANTS

INDEX OF ADVERTISERS